STARGAZING 2009

MONTH-BY-MONTH GUIDE TO THE NORTHERN NIGHT SKY

HEATHER COUPER & NIGEL HENBEST

HEATHER COUPER and NIGEL HENBEST are internationally recognized writers and broadcasters on astronomy, space and science. They have written more than 30 books and over 1000 articles, and are the founders of an independent TV production company specializing in factual and scientific programming.

Heather is a past President of both the British Astronomical Association and the Society for Popular Astronomy. She is a Fellow of the Royal Astronomical Society, a Fellow of the Institute of Physics and a former Millennium Commissioner, for which she was awarded the CBE in 2007. Nigel has been Astronomy Consultant to *New Scientist* magazine, Editor of the *Journal of the British Astronomical Association* and Media Consultant to the Royal Greenwich Observatory.

Published in Great Britain in 2008 by Philip's,
a division of Octopus Publishing Group Limited
(www.octopusbooks.co.uk)
2–4 Heron Quays, London E14 4JP
An Hachette UK Company (www.hachettelivre.co.uk)

Reprinted 2009

TEXT
Heather Couper and Nigel Henbest (pages 6–53)
Robin Scagell (pages 61–64)
Philip's (pages 1–5, 54–60)

ISBN 978–0–540–09314–4

Printed in China

Details of other Philip's titles and services can be found on our website at: **www.philips-maps.co.uk**

Title page: Rosette Nebula (Nick King/Galaxy)

ACKNOWLEDGEMENTS
All star maps by Wil Tirion/Philip's, with extra annotation by Philip's.
Artworks © Philip's.

All photographs courtesy Galaxy Picture Library:
David Cortner *8;*
Eddie Guscott *36, 44;*
James Jefferson *24;*
Nick King *16, 33;*
Pete Lawrence *49;*
Thierry Legault *21;*
Damian Peach *63;*
Robin Scagell *12, 28, 40, 61, 62, 64;*
Michael Stecker *52.*

CONTENTS

The sight of diamond-bright stars sparkling against a sky of black velvet is one of life's most glorious experiences. No wonder stargazing is so popular. Learning your way around the night sky requires nothing more than patience, a reasonably clear sky and the 12 star charts included in this book.

Stargazing 2009 is a guide to the sky for every month of the year. Complete beginners will find it an essential night-time companion, while seasoned amateur astronomers will find the updates invaluable.

THE MONTHLY CHARTS

Each pair of monthly charts shows the views of the heavens looking north and south. They are usable throughout most of Europe – between 40 and 60 degrees north. Only the brightest stars are shown (otherwise we would have had to put 3000 stars on each chart, instead of about 200). This means that we plot stars down to 3rd magnitude, with a few 4th-magnitude stars to complete distinctive patterns. We also show the ecliptic, which is the apparent path of the Sun in the sky.

USING THE STAR CHARTS

To use the charts, begin by locating the north Pole Star – Polaris – by using the stars of the Plough (see March). When you are looking at Polaris you are facing north, with west on your left and east on your right. (West and east are reversed on star charts because they show the view looking up into the sky instead of down towards the ground.) The left-hand chart then shows the view you have to the north. Most of the stars you see will be circumpolar, which means that they are visible all year. The other stars rise in the east and set in the west.

Now turn and face the opposite direction, south. This is the view that changes most during the course of the year. Leo, with its prominent 'sickle' formation, is high in the spring skies. Summer is dominated by the bright trio of Vega, Deneb and Altair. Autumn's familiar marker is the Square of Pegasus, while the winter sky is ruled over by the stars of Orion.

The charts show the sky as it appears in the late evening for each month: the exact times are noted in the caption with the chart. If you are observing in the early morning, you will find that the view is different. As a rule of thumb, if you are observing two hours later than the time suggested in the caption, then the following month's map will more accurately represent the stars on view. So, if you wish to observe at midnight in the middle of February, two hours later than the time suggested in the caption, then the stars will appear as they are on March's chart. When using a chart for the 'wrong' month, however, bear in mind that the planets and Moon will not be shown in their correct positions.

THE MOON, PLANETS AND SPECIAL EVENTS

In addition to the stars visible each month, the charts show the positions of any planets on view in the late evening. Other planets may also be visible that month, but they will not be on the chart if they have already set, or if they do not rise until early morning. Their positions are described in the text, so that you can find them if you are observing at other times.

We have also plotted the path of the Moon. Its position is marked at three-day intervals. The dates when it reaches First Quarter, Full Moon, Last Quarter and New Moon are given in the text. If there is a meteor shower in the month, we mark the position from which the meteors appear to emanate – the *radiant*. More information on observing the planets and other Solar System objects is given on pages 54–57.

Once you have identified the constellations and found the planets, you will want to know more about what's on view. Each month, we explain one object, such as a particularly interesting star or galaxy, in detail. We have also chosen a spectacular image for each month and described how it was captured. All of these pictures were taken by amateurs. We list details and dates of special events, such as meteor showers or eclipses, and give observing tips. Finally, each month we pick a topic related to what's on view, ranging from the Milky Way to double stars and space missions, and discuss it in more detail. Where possible, all relevant objects are highlighted on the maps.

FURTHER INFORMATION

The year's star charts form the heart of the book, providing material for many enjoyable observing sessions. For background information turn to pages 54–57, where diagrams help to explain, among other things, the movement of the planets and why we see eclipses.

Although there is plenty to see with the naked eye, many observers use binoculars or telescopes, and some choose to record their observations using cameras, CCDs or webcams. For a round-up of what's new in observing technology, go to pages 61–64, where equipment expert Robin Scagell shares his knowledge.

If you have already invested in binoculars or a telescope, then you can explore the deep sky – nebulae (starbirth sites), star clusters and galaxies. On pages 58–60 we list recommended deep-sky objects, constellation by constellation. Use the appropriate month's maps to see which constellations are on view, and then choose your targets. The table of 'limiting magnitude' (page 58) will help you to decide if a particular object is visible with your equipment.

Happy stargazing!

Welcome to the International Year of Astronomy (IYA)! All over the world, people will be celebrating our glorious heavens during 2009. Look out for special events in March, July and October that everyone can get involved in. The peg is that it's 400 years since Galileo turned his 'optick tube' towards the sky, and made his astonishing discoveries. But was he the *first* to use an astronomical telescope? Probably not – see July.

▼ The sky at 10 pm in mid-January, with Moon positions at three-day intervals either side of Full Moon. The star positions are also correct for 11 pm at

JANUARY'S CONSTELLATION

Crowned by glorious **Sirius**, the brightest star in the sky, **Canis Major** is the larger of **Orion**'s two hunting dogs. He is represented as chasing **Lepus** (the Hare), a very faint constellation below Orion, but his main target is Orion's chief quarry, **Taurus** (the Bull) – take a line from Sirius through Orion's belt and you'll spot the celestial bovine on the other side. From Britain, 'the Greater Dog' is too low in the sky to be a brilliant sight. But Arabian astronomers, at lower latitudes, accorded great importance to Canis Major. Without fail, they saw the constellation as a dog. The Indians regarded both cosmic dogs (**Canis Minor** lies to the left of Orion) as being 'watchdogs of the Milky Way' – which runs between the two constellations.

To the right of Sirius is the star **Mirzam**, whose Arabic name means 'the Announcer' – the presence of Mirzam heralded the appearance of Sirius, one of the most venerated stars in the sky. Just below Sirius is a beautiful star cluster, **M41**. This loose agglomeration of over a hundred young stars – 2500 light years away – is easily visible through binoculars, and even to the unaided eye. It's rumoured that the Greek philosopher Aristotle, in 325 BC, called it 'a cloudy spot' – the earliest description of a deep-sky object.

the beginning of January, and 9 pm at the end of the month. The planets move slightly relative to the stars during the month.

PLANETS ON VIEW

There's quite a grouping of planets low in the south-west after sunset – though they all set too early to show on our chart, and some will be difficult to spot in the twilight glow. By far the most prominent is brilliant **Venus** (magnitude −4.4), hanging like a tiny lamp in the south-western sky in the constellation Aquarius. It's at greatest eastern elongation on 14 January. At the start of the month, Venus sets at 8.15 pm; by the end of January, the Evening Star graces our evening sky until 9.20 pm.

Distant **Uranus** is also skulking in Aquarius, on the edge of naked-eye visibility at magnitude +5.9; it sinks below the horizon around 9.25 pm. Fast-moving Venus passes Uranus on the evening of 22 January. This is an excellent opportunity to spot the dim planet: Uranus lies about a degree to the left of Venus, and is brighter than any of the stars in the vicinity – even though it's 10,000 times fainter than Venus!

On the first few evenings of 2009, you may just catch **Jupiter** very low in the south-west after the Sun sets, shining at magnitude −1.9. On 1 January, fainter **Mercury** (magnitude −0.6) lies just to its left. As Jupiter sinks into the sunset, Mercury remains visible for the first two weeks of the year: it reaches greatest eastern elongation on 4 January, when it sets at 5.45 pm.

Between Venus and Mercury, you'll find **Neptune** (magnitude +8.0) in Capricornus, setting at around 7 pm.

Star chart labels

WEST

2 Jan

PISCES

TRIANGULUM

PERSEUS

Algol

Zeta

Capella

Zenith

AURIGA

URSA MAJOR

Castor

Pollux

The Sickle

Regulus

LEO

VIRGO

Saturn

Ecliptic

EAST

ARIES

Pleiades

5 Jan

8 Jan

Aldebaran

TAURUS

ORION

Betelgeuse

GEMINI

11 Jan

CANCER

14 Jan

Procyon

CANIS MINOR

HYDRA

Mira

CETUS

Rigel

ERIDANUS

LEPUS

Sirius

M41

CANIS MAJOR

Mirzam

Adhara

COLUMBA

PUPPIS

THE MILKY WAY

SOUTH

SE

MS

January's Object
Pleiades

Radiant of
Quadrantids

Saturn

Moon

MOON

Date	Time	Phase
4	11.56 am	First Quarter
11	3.27 am	Full Moon
18	2.46 am	Last Quarter
26	7.55 am	New Moon

Away from all this twilight activity, **Saturn** rises in the east around 10.30 pm. Shining at magnitude +0.9, the ringed planet lies on the borders of Leo and Virgo.

Mars is lost in the Sun's glare all this month.

MOON

The crescent Moon lies 4 degrees above Uranus on the evening of 2 January. On the evening of 7 January it passes right in front of the Pleiades (see Special Events). The Moon passes Saturn on the night of 14/15 January. The evening of 27 January sees the thin crescent Moon only a degree to the right of Neptune – a challenge to observe in the twilight! The Moon passes Venus between 29 and 30 January.

SPECIAL EVENTS

The maximum of the **Quadrantid** meteor shower occurs on **3/4 January**. These shooting stars are tiny particles of dust shed by an old comet called 2003 EH1, burning up as they enter the Earth's atmosphere. Perspective makes them appear to emanate from one spot in the sky, the *radiant* (marked on the star chart).

On **4 January**, the Earth is at perihelion, its closest point to the Sun.

As it gets dark on **7 January**, you can spot the Moon moving right in front of the Seven Sisters – the Pleiades star cluster (see January's Object). Which stars are hidden, and the exact timing, depends on your location. The occultation of the brighter 'sisters' starts around 4.15 pm, and the occultations end around 6.30 pm. The event is best seen in binoculars or a small telescope.

We won't see it from the UK, but on **26 January** there's an annular eclipse of the Sun – where the Moon moves right in front of the Sun, but appears smaller so that a bright ring (*annulus*) of the Sun's surface remains visible. You need to be in the Indian Ocean or Indonesia to see the annular eclipse; a partial eclipse is visible in southern Africa and western Australia.

JANUARY'S OBJECT

The **Pleiades** star cluster is one of the most familiar sky-sights. Though it's well known as the Seven Sisters, most people

⊙ Viewing tip

It may sound obvious, but if you want to stargaze at this most glorious time of year, dress up warmly! Lots of layers are better than a heavy coat, as they trap air next to your skin – and heavy-soled boots will stop the frost creeping up your legs. It may sound anorakish, but a woolly hat really does stop one-third of your body's heat escaping through the top of your head. And, alas, no hipflask of whisky – alcohol constricts the veins and will make you feel even colder.

see any number of stars but seven! Most people can pick out the six brightest stars, while very keen-sighted observers can discern up to 11 stars. These are just the most luminous in a group of 500 stars, lying about 400 light years away (although there's an ongoing debate about the precise distance!). The brightest stars in the Pleiades are hot and blue, and all the stars are young – less than 80 million years old. They were all born together, and have yet to go their separate ways. The fledgling stars have blundered into a cloud of gas in space, which looks like gossamer on webcam images. Even to the unaided eye or through binoculars, they are a beautiful sight.

JANUARY'S PICTURE

Although the Moon and the Sun appear – by an amazing coincidence – to be the same size in the sky, the Moon's elliptical orbit around the Earth can take it further away. At these times, during an eclipse of the Sun, the Moon can't quite overlap the Sun's disc – leaving an *annulus* ('ring') of light around our local star. In the future, the Moon will drift away from the Earth and annular eclipses will become more common than total eclipses – so we'll miss out on seeing the fireworks of the Sun's outer atmosphere.

◄ *This view by David Cortner of the annular eclipse of 24 December 1973 in Costa Rica shows how this month's eclipse may appear at sunset from Indonesia. He used a 3½ inch (90 mm) Questar at f/15 on Kodachome-II colour film and a Nikon F2 camera. The exposure was ¹/₂₀₀₀ second through a deep-red filter.*

JANUARY'S TOPIC
Venus

As the Evening Star, Venus is unmissable this month. The planet of love is undeniably beautiful – it's pure white, and so brilliant that it can cast a shadow. But appearances are deceptive. Venus – almost the Earth's twin in size – is cloaked in dense clouds of sulphuric acid, which reflect sunlight so efficiently that the planet literally dazzles.

Probe under those clouds, however, and you discover a world that has gone badly wrong. One commentator noted that – if you landed on Venus – you'd be simultaneously crushed, corroded, suffocated, and roasted.

Crushed? That's the atmospheric pressure – 90 times that of the Earth's. Corroded? Blame the sulphuric-acid rain in the upper atmosphere. Suffocated? Well – you can't breathe its carbon dioxide atmosphere. Roasted? Our next-neighbour-world – two out from the Sun – is the hottest in the Solar System. With a surface boasting a temperature of 460°C, Venus is fiercer than an oven.

Almost certainly, active volcanoes are to blame, dumping vast amounts of carbon dioxide into the planet's atmosphere and leading to a runaway 'greenhouse effect'. But Venus is a salutary example to *us* to reduce our carbon dioxide and methane footprints – which are of our own making.

The first signs of spring are on the way, as the winter star-patterns start to drift towards the west, setting earlier. The constantly changing pageant of constellations in the sky is proof that we live on a cosmic merry-go-round, orbiting the Sun. Imagine it: you're in the fairground, circling the Mighty Wurlitzer on your horse, and looking out around you. At times you spot the ghost train; sometimes you see the roller-coaster; and then you swing past the candy-floss stall. So it is with the sky – and the constellations – as we circle our local star. That's why we get to see different stars in different seasons.

FEBRUARY'S CONSTELLATION

It has to be **Orion** – the most recognizable constellation in the sky. And it's one of the rare star-groupings that really looks like its namesake – a giant of a man with a sword below his belt, wielding a club above his head. Orion is fabled in mythology as the ultimate hunter.

Orion is truly one of the jewels of the night sky. It contains one-tenth of the brightest stars in the sky: Orion's seven main stars all lie in the 'top 70' of brilliant stars. Despite its distinctive shape, most of these stars are not closely associated with each other: they simply line up, one behind the other, as we look down the length of a minor spiral arm in our Milky Way Galaxy – fittingly known as the 'Orion Arm'.

Closest to us is the star that forms the hunter's upper right shoulder, **Bellatrix**, at 240 light years distance. Next up is blood-red **Betelgeuse**, at the top left of Orion. The constellation's second brightest star, Betelgeuse is 430 light years away. It's a cool, bloated, dying star – known as a red giant – over 300 times the size of the Sun.

The constellation's brightest star, blue-white **Rigel**, could hardly be more different. It's a vigorous young star more than twice as hot as our Sun (its surface temperature is around

▼ *The sky at 10 pm in mid-February, with Moon positions at three-day intervals either side of Full Moon. The star positions are also correct for 11 pm at*

EAST

the beginning of February, and 9 pm at the end of the month. The planets move slightly relative to the stars during the month.

12,000°C), and Rigel is more than 50,000 times as bright. It lies 800 light years from us, roughly the same distance as the star that marks the other corner of Orion's tunic – **Saiph** – and the two outer stars of the belt, **Alnitak** (left) and **Mintaka** (right).

We must travel 1300 light years from home to reach the middle star of the belt, **Alnilam**. And at the same distance, we find the stars of the 'sword' hanging below the belt, which is the lair of the great **Orion Nebula** (see December's Object).

PLANETS ON VIEW

Venus is queen of the evening sky. Blazing at magnitude −4.6, it's 15 times more brilliant than the brightest star, Sirius. Mid-month, it's setting about four hours after the Sun. Through a small telescope, you'll see Venus growing larger and changing in shape from a half-lit ball to a crescent as it approaches the Earth.

Uranus is just visible low in the south-west, at magnitude +5.9 in Aquarius; by the end of February it has sunk into the twilight glow.

Rising in the east at around 7.15 pm, **Saturn** lies between the constellations of Leo and Virgo, shining at magnitude +0.6. The ringed planet will be at its closest to Earth early next month.

In the morning sky, you may just catch **Mercury** (magnitude +0.1) for the first two weeks of February, very low in the south-east in the dawn twilight. The innermost planet is at greatest western elongation on 13 February, and then quickly drops out of sight into the horizon glow.

WEST

PISCES
CETUS
PERSEUS
3 Feb
TAURUS
Pleiades
Aldebaran
ERIDANUS
LEPUS
Bellatrix
Mintaka
Alnilam
Rigel
ORION
Alnitak
Saiph
Mirzam
M35
AURIGA
Castor
GEMINI
Betelgeuse
Orion Nebula
Sirius
CANIS MAJOR
Capella
Pollux
6 Feb
Procyon
Adhara
Zenith
CANCER
CANIS MINOR
THE MILKY WAY
URSA MAJOR
The Sickle
9 Feb
HYDRA
PUPPIS
LEO
Regulus
VIRGO
Saturn
12 Feb
Ecliptic
SOUTH
SE

EAST

MOON		
Date	Time	Phase
2	11.13 pm	First Quarter
9	2.49 pm	Full Moon
16	9.37 pm	Last Quarter
25	1.35 am	New Moon

February's Object
Sirius

February's Picture
M35

Saturn

Moon

11

Jupiter, Mars and **Neptune** are too close to the Sun to be visible this month.

▲ *This shot of M35 was a single 15-second exposure taken by Robin Scagell using a Canon 10D digital camera at ISO 800 through a 400 mm telephoto lens.*

MOON

On the morning of 4 February, the Moon occults the Pleiades (see Special Events). It passes below Saturn on the night of 10/11 February. The thin crescent Moon forms a lovely sight in the sky with Venus on the evenings of 27 and 28 February.

SPECIAL EVENTS

Following January's occultation of the Pleiades, there's a repeat of the phenomenon in the early morning of **4 February**, though very low in the north-western sky. The first of the brighter stars in the Seven Sisters is hidden at 2.10 am, while the final star reappears at 4.20. You'll need to live in the north of Scotland to see the full show; further south, the Moon and Pleiades will set while the Moon is right in front of the star cluster.

FEBRUARY'S OBJECT

This is the month of the brightest star in the sky – **Sirius**. It isn't a particularly luminous star: it just happens to lie nearby, at a distance of 8.6 light years. 'The Dog Star' is accompanied by a little companion, affectionately called 'the Pup'. This tiny star was discovered in 1862 by Alvan Clark when he was testing a telescope, but it had been predicted by Friedrich Bessel nearly 20 years before, when he'd observed that something was

Viewing tip

When you first go out to observe, you may be disappointed at how few stars you can see in the sky. But wait for around 20 minutes, and you'll be amazed at how your night vision improves. One reason for this 'dark adaption' is that the pupil of your eye gets larger to make the best of the darkness. More importantly, in dark conditions the retina of your eye builds up much bigger reserves of rhodopsin, the chemical that responds to light.

'tugging' on Sirius. The Pup is a white dwarf – the dying nuclear reactor of an ancient star which has puffed off its atmosphere. White dwarfs are the size of a planet, but have the mass of a star: because they're so collapsed, they have considerable gravitational powers – hence Sirius' wobble. The Pup is visible through medium-powered telescopes.

FEBRUARY'S PICTURE

The open cluster **M35** in Gemini is a favourite with amateur astronomers. This swarm of around 500 stars is about 2800 light years away, and is visible to the unaided eye. It covers an area as large as the Full Moon. If you have a reasonable telescope, look to the south-west of M35 to spot NGC 2158 – a much more ancient cluster which lies at a distance of 16,000 light years.

FEBRUARY'S TOPIC
Star Names

Why do the brightest stars have such strange names? The reason is that they date from antiquity, and have passed on down generations ever since. The original western star names – like the original constellations – were probably Babylonian or Chaldean, but few of these survive. The Greeks took up the baton after that, and the name of the star **Antares** (see June's Object) is a direct result. It means 'rival of Ares' because its red colour rivals that of the planet Mars (*Ares* in Greek).

The Romans were not particularly interested in astronomy, but nevertheless left their mark on the sky. **Capella**, the brightest star of Auriga, has Roman roots: the name is a diminutive of *capra* (goat), and it literally means 'the little she-goat' (a bit of an understatement for a star over 100 times brighter than the Sun).

But the Arabs were largely responsible for the star names we have inherited today. Working in the so-called 'Dark Ages' between the 6th and 10th centuries AD, they took over the naming of the sky – hence the number of stars beginning with the letters 'al' (Arabic for 'the'). **Algol**, in the constellation Perseus, means 'the demon' – possibly because the Arabs noticed that its brightness seems to 'wink' every few days. **Deneb**, in Cygnus, also has Arabic roots – it means 'the tail' (of the flying bird).

But the most remembered star name in the sky is Orion's **Betelgeuse**. For some time, it was gloriously interpreted as 'the armpit of the sacred one'. But the 'B' in Betelgeuse turned out to be a mistranslation – and so we're none the wiser as to how our distant ancestors really identified this fiery red star.

The first of the International Year of Astronomy's star parties kicks off this month, with 'Moonwatch Week' starting on 28 March. Contact your local astronomical society to have the chance to range over our satellite's rugged terrain through a powerful telescope. And – while you're there – don't miss a close-up of ringworld **Saturn**, at its closest to the Earth this month.

▼ The sky at 10 pm in mid-March, with Moon positions at three-day intervals either side of Full Moon. The star positions are also correct for 11 pm at

MARCH'S CONSTELLATION

Ursa Major – whose brightest stars are usually called **'the Plough'** – ties with Orion as being the most famous constellation. Orion's fame is clear to see: its stars are brilliant, and make up a very powerful image of a giant dominating the sky. In contrast, those of the Plough are fainter, and most people today have probably never seen an old-fashioned horse-drawn plough, from which the constellation takes its name. In fact, some children call it 'the sauce-pan', while in America it's known as 'the Big Dipper'.

But the Plough is the first constellation that most people get to know. There are two reasons. First, the two end stars of the 'bowl' of the Plough point directly towards the Pole Star: also known as **Polaris**, it's the star that lies directly above the Earth's North Pole. As the Earth spins on its axis, the stars rise and set, while the Pole Star stays still – because we are actually rotating *under* the Pole Star. Locating the Pole Star is a sure way to find the direction of north. And because the Plough is so close to Polaris, it never sets as seen from northern latitudes – which is why it is such a familiar sight.

The seven stars of the Plough are quite a rarity: unlike most constellations, several of the stars lie at the same distance and were born together. The middle five stars are all moving in the same direction (along with brilliant **Sirius**, which is also a member of the group). Over thousands

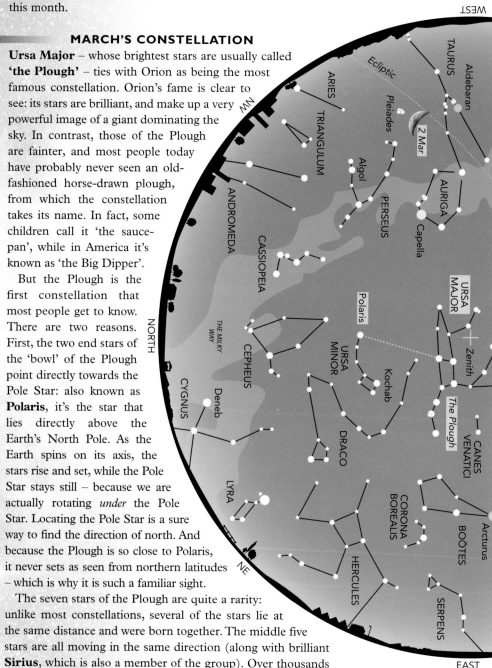

the beginning of March, and 10 pm at the end of the month (after BST begins). The planets move slightly relative to the stars during the month.

of years, the shape of the Plough will gradually change, as the two 'end' stars go off on their own paths.

PLANETS ON VIEW

March is the last month in 2009 when we'll see **Venus** in all its splendour as an Evening Star, after months of glory queening it over the western sky. Though Venus begins the month as prominent as ever – at magnitude −4.6 and setting three-and-a-half hours after the Sun – by the end of March it's dropped right out of sight. Through a small telescope, watch Venus grow ever bigger and its illuminated portion thin to a narrow crescent.

As it disappears from the evening sky, Venus is born again – as the Morning Star. For a few days before Venus passes the Sun on 27 March, you may be able to spot the planet in both the evening and the morning sky! Immediately after sunset, scan just to the right of the point where the Sun has gone down with good binoculars or a small telescope; and – in the morning – scan the horizon to the east around 5.30 am. *Stop observing the instant the Sun rises, so you don't inadvertently scan across its blinding surface.*

Also in the morning sky, by the end of the month you'll catch **Jupiter** (magnitude −2.1) low in the twilight well to the right of Venus.

The 'star' of the evening sky is **Saturn**: at magnitude +0.5, it's visible all night long under the tail of Leo (the Lion). The ringed planet is at opposition on 8 March,

WEST

Aldebaran
TAURUS
ERIDANUS
Rigel
ORION
Betelgeuse
Rosette Nebula
LEPUS
Sirius
MS
AURIGA
GEMINI
5 Mar
Castor
Pollux
Procyon
CANIS MINOR
THE MILKY WAY
CANIS MAJOR
PUPPIS
CANCER
8 Mar
URSA MAJOR
Zenith
Regulus
HYDRA
SOUTH
The Sickle
LEO
Saturn
11 Mar
CANES VENATICI
Denebola
CORVUS
BOÖTES
Arcturus
VIRGO
Spica
Ecliptic
SERPENS
SE
EAST

March's Object
Saturn
March's Picture
Rosette Nebula

Saturn

Moon

MOON		
Date	**Time**	**Phase**
4	7.46 am	First Quarter
11	2.38 am	Full Moon
18	5.47 pm	Last Quarter
26	4.06 pm	New Moon

when it's opposite the Sun in the sky, and at its closest point to Earth this year. Take this opportunity to train a small telescope on Saturn's largest moon, Titan (see Special Events), and the famous rings, which at the moment appear very thin as we're seeing them at a very shallow angle.

Mercury, Mars, Uranus and **Neptune** are too close to the Sun to be seen this month.

MOON

The almost-Full Moon lies near to Saturn on 10 March. In the early morning of 17 March, the Moon passes only half a degree below Antares, the bright red giant star in Scorpius. Just before sunrise on 22 and 23 March, the crescent Moon lies close to Jupiter.

SPECIAL EVENTS

If you're checking **Saturn** on **4 March** through a telescope, the brightest object nearby is not its biggest moon Titan, as you might expect, but a background star. Catalogued as HD 98697, it shines at magnitude +6.7 – four times brighter than Titan (magnitude +8.2).

The Vernal Equinox, on **20 March** at 11.43 am, marks the beginning of spring, as the Sun moves up to shine over the northern hemisphere.

28 March–**5 April** is Moonwatch Week (Spring), part of the International Year of Astronomy celebrations. Organized star parties will be homing in on the Moon and Saturn.

29 March, 1.00 am: British Summer Time starts – don't forget to put your clocks forward (the mnemonic is 'spring forward, fall back').

MARCH'S OBJECT

Ringworld **Saturn** is currently skulking under Leo's tail. Famed for its huge engirdling appendages – the rings would stretch nearly all the way from the Earth to the Moon – you'll be hard-pressed to see them this year, because they're presented almost edge-on.

And the rings are just the beginnings of Saturn's larger family. It has at least 60 moons, including Titan – where Europe's Huygens probe recently discovered lakes of liquid methane and ethane.

Saturn itself is second only to Jupiter in size. But it's so low in density, that, were you to plop it in an ocean, it would float. Like Jupiter, it shares a ferocious spin rate – 10 hours and 32 minutes – and has wind speeds of up to 1800 km/h.

Saturn's atmosphere is much blander than that of its larger cousin. But it's wracked with lightning-bolts 1000 times more powerful than those on Earth.

And, roughly every 30 years – its rotation period around the Sun – Saturn breaks out in white spots. This coincides with summer in Saturn's northern hemisphere – so you can expect the next rash in about 2020.

MARCH'S PICTURE

The glorious **Rosette Nebula** is a true celestial gem. Some 5000 light years away, the petals of the rose spread out over 130 light years of space. Baby stars are being born in the nebula today, their violent radiation and winds punching a hole in the nebula's heart. Researchers calculate that the Rosette is capable of giving birth to 10,000 stars.

▼ *The Rosette Nebula in Monoceros, photographed by Nick King from Harrow, Middlesex, using a Takahashi FS102 refracting telescope at f/5.9, with a Starlight Xpress SXV-Hp CCD camera. A combination of 70 minutes of separate exposures through filters.*

MARCH'S TOPIC
The Equinox

On Jersey, there's a huge burial mound: La Hougue Bie. On top of the mound is a chapel, lined up so that the chancel – like churches all over Britain – faces east. In 1924, archaeologists excavated the mound and discovered a long passage grave. It, too, faces east.

The tradition of east–west alignments goes back to the dawn of antiquity. For it was then that day and night were equal (hence 'equinox'): the Sun rose due east, and set due west. These were important times of year for farming communities, marking the start of spring, and the onset of autumn, respectively.

Because of the Earth's skewed axis – 23½ degrees to its orbit around the Sun – its tilt favours the southern hemisphere between September and March (when the Antipodeans delight in summer), while the opposite is true in the northern hemisphere. In mid-March and mid-September, the Sun hovers above the equator, creating the symmetry that causes the equinoxes.

Our ancestors celebrated these punctuation marks in the year – such as the solstices in December and June, when the Sun appeared at its lowest and at its highest in the sky. Stonehenge, in Wiltshire, is a monumental shrine to the solstices, set in tablets of stone.

La Hougue Bie, on the other hand, is aligned with the equinoxes. In March and September, the rising Sun shines directly on to the east end of the chapel. And a shaft of sunlight pierces the heart of the tomb below.

Spring is here, with the skies dominated by the ancient constellations of **Leo** and **Virgo**. Leo does indeed look like a recumbent lion, but it's hard to envisage Y-shaped Virgo as a maiden holding an ear of corn!

APRIL'S CONSTELLATION

Hydra (the Water Snake) is the largest constellation in the sky – it's about 100° long, which means that it straggles over a quarter of the heavens. But Hydra is hardly spectacular. If you live in a light-polluted city, you'll search for it in vain.

Country-dwellers are in with a chance. Look below the stars of **Leo** and ringworld **Saturn** (under Leo's tail), and you'll trace out the convoluted line of faint stars that make up what was – evidently – a fearsome beast.

In legend, the superhero Hercules had to slay Hydra as one of his 12 'labours' – a penance after he had murdered his wife and children. But killing the Hydra was not an easy task. First, the Water Snake was so fearsome that even strong men died of fright when they saw it. And it had numerous heads – and if one was chopped off, three would grow back! Hercules hacked away the extra heads, cauterizing the stumps with burning bushes. Finally, he severed the final immortal head with his sword.

In the heavens, Hydra's head is nothing more than a pretty group of faint stars below the constellation of Cancer. The constellation's major star is second-magnitude **Alphard** – meaning 'the solitary one'.

If you have a small telescope, try to find Hydra's hidden glory. Look under the tail of the serpentine beast, and you'll spot an 8th-magnitude fuzzy blur. It's **M83** – one of the most glorious, face-on spiral galaxies in the sky.

And if you haven't got a telescope, log on to find an image of

▼ The sky at 11 pm in mid-April, with Moon positions at three-day intervals either side of Full Moon. The star positions are also correct for midnight at the beginning of

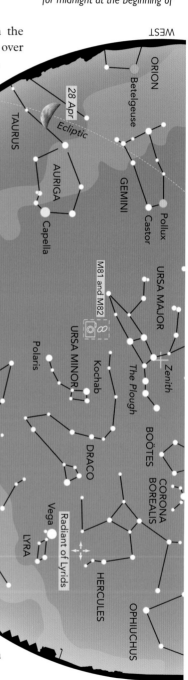

April, and 10 pm at the end of the month. The planets move slightly relative to the stars during the month.

M83 on the European Southern Observatory website. You won't be disappointed.

PLANETS ON VIEW

This is the month to see elusive **Mercury** putting on its best evening show in 2009: it's at greatest eastern elongation on 26 April. Between 10 April and the end of the month, look low down between west and north-west, just as the sky is growing dark. Once you spot it, Mercury is surprising bright – it's just that we never see it in a dark sky. Around 10 April, Mercury is magnitude −1.3, almost equal to the brightest star, Sirius. By the end of April, it fades to magnitude +1.1, and lies near the Pleiades (see Special Events).

Saturn is shining all night long under the hindquarters of Leo, at magnitude +0.7. A small telescope shows its rings, seen almost edge-on, and its biggest moon, Titan.

Giant planet **Jupiter** (magnitude −2.2) is creeping upwards in the dawn twilight, low in the southeast in Capricornus. At the beginning of April it rises at 5.10 am, and as early as 3.30 am by the end of the month. A small telescope reveals its four main moons – sometimes with an interloper . . . (see Special Events).

Brighter **Venus** follows Jupiter in the morning sky, lying some way to the left. It rises at 5.40 am at the start of April, and 4.10 am by the month's end. Starting the month at magnitude −4.1, it brightens during April to −4.4. Through a small telescope,

WEST

THE MILKY WAY

GEMINI

Procyon

CANIS MINOR

Castor

Pollux

3 Apr

CANCER

Alphard

Regulus

HYDRA

URSA MAJOR

The Sickle

LEO

Saturn 6 Apr

M65/M66 NGC 3628

CORVUS

Zenith

CANES VENATICI

Porrima

Arcturus

Spica 9 Apr

M83

The Plough

BOÖTES

VIRGO

Ecliptic

CORONA BOREALIS

SERPENS

LIBRA

HERCULES

OPHIUCHUS

SE

EAST

SOUTH

SW

April's Objects
M65, M66 and
NGC 3628

April's Picture
M81 and M82

Saturn

Moon

	MOON		
Date	Time	Phase	
2	3.34 pm	First Quarter	
9	3.56 pm	Full Moon	
17	2.36 pm	Last Quarter	
25	4.22 am	New Moon	

you'll see its crescent shape grow fatter, and the planet smaller, as Venus pulls away from the Earth.

Mars, **Uranus** and **Neptune** are all lost in the bright morning twilight.

MOON

The Moon passes near Regulus, in Leo, on 5 April, and Saturn on 6 April. It lies near Virgo's brightest star, Spica, on 9 April. In the early morning of 19 and 20 April, the Moon is near Jupiter. Back in the evening sky, the Moon is near Mercury and the Pleiades on 26 April (see Special Events).

SPECIAL EVENTS

21/22 April: It's the maximum of the **Lyrid** meteor shower, which – by perspective – appear to emanate from the constellation of Lyra. The shower, which consists of particles from Comet Thatcher, is active between 19 and 25 April. This is a good year to observe the Lyrids as the Moon is out of the way.

On the mornings of **25–28 April**, telescope users are in for a treat, as Jupiter appears to have five bright moons: the interloper is the star 44 Capricorni (magnitude +5.9). At 5.10 am on **26 April**, the star lies only 5 arcseconds from Ganymede (magnitude +5.3).

There's a spectacular grouping very low in the west-north-west after sunset on **26 April**, when the very thin crescent Moon lies on the outskirts of the Pleiades (the Seven Sisters), with Mercury just below.

On **29** and **30 April**, Mercury moves through the fringes of the Pleiades – best seen with binoculars or a small telescope.

APRIL'S OBJECTS

Look under **Leo**'s tummy to see a pair of spiral galaxies – **M65** and **M66** – which lie around 30 million light years away. They're *just* visible through binoculars, but you'll need a telescope to glimpse **NGC 3628**, the third member of the 'Leo Triplet'. This month, you'll find them about 5 degrees above Saturn.

The trio make up a small cluster of galaxies, probably similar to our own 'Local Group'. Like our Local Group, the cluster must harbour dozens of dwarf galaxies, too faint to be seen.

M65 and NGC 3628 are both seen edge-on, so we can't ascertain much of their structure. But M66 – the brightest of the trio at magnitude +8.9 – comes at you full-frontal. It's a glorious galaxy, with curving arms caressing a brilliant nucleus.

Theory has it that NGC 3628 and M66 had a close encounter in the past. The interaction left a legacy: NGC 3628 is crossed with a dark band of cosmic dust – a maternity ward for the formation of new stars. M66 has a brilliant nucleus – a

⊙ **Viewing tip**

Don't think that you need a telescope to bring the heavens closer. Binoculars are excellent – and you can fling them into the back of the car at the last minute. But when you buy binoculars, make sure that you get those with the biggest lenses, coupled with a modest magnification. Binoculars are described, for instance, as being '7 x 50' – meaning that the magnification is seven times, and that the diameter of the lenses is 50 mm across. These are ideal for astronomy – they have good light grasp, and the low magnification means that they don't exaggerate the wobbles of your arms too much. It's always best to rest your binoculars on a wall or a fence to steady the image. Some amateurs are the lucky owners of huge binoculars – say, 20 x 70 – with which you can see the rings of Saturn (being so large, these need a special mounting). But above all, *never* buy binoculars with small lenses that promise huge magnifications – they're a total waste of money.

▲ The galaxies M81 and M82 can be seen using binoculars, but this detailed view of the pair was taken from France by Thierry Legault using a Takahashi TOA-130 f/7.7 refractor with Canon 10D digital camera. He added 29 exposures of 5 minutes at 400 ISO.

sign that the entanglement between the two galaxies has already generated starbirth.

APRIL'S PICTURE

One of Ursa Major's secrets: the galaxies **M81** and **M82**. These are two members of a galaxy cluster – similar in size to our Local Group – which lies a 'mere' 12 million light years away. Both galaxies are raising cosmic tides on each other. M81 (right) is a serene spiral, exhibiting little signs of ethereal altercation. But for M82 (left), it's a different matter. The interaction between the two galaxies has provoked a violent reaction at the core of this edge-on spiral, leading to a fury of star formation.

APRIL'S TOPIC
Light Pollution

We once received a letter from a lady in Kent, saying: 'Before the War, we could see so many stars. But they're not there any more. Have they faded?' No – light pollution is the culprit. Our skies are crammed with particles of dust, coming from sources like car exhausts and factory emissions. Couple this with badly-designed streetlighting – and, hey presto, the stars disappear. It's not just an aesthetic issue. It's calculated that Britain throws away £52 million and two power-stations-worth of energy a year in badly-designed lighting. It is robbing us of our vision of the skies – and contributing to global warming. It isn't even making our lives any safer from crime, for research shows that more crimes are committed in well-lit areas. What's to be done? The Clean Neighbourhoods Act, which addresses (among other nuisances) noise and light pollution, should make a difference. And lighting engineers are actively working on new designs for streetlights that point the light down, and not up. We hope this will bring us our vision of the dark night sky again. Otherwise, the only recourse will be to sit under the artificial skies of a planetarium.

Look south to find the red giant **Arcturus** – 'the Bearkeeper'. It's the brightest star in the constellation of **Boötes** (the Herdsman), who shepherds the two bears through the heavens. Next to Boötes is the beautiful coronet of **Corona Borealis**. Its brightest star – sparkling in the crown's centre – is appropriately called **Gemma**.

MAY'S CONSTELLATION

For one of antiquity's superheroes, the celestial version of **Hercules** looks like a wimp. While Orion is all strutting masculinity, Hercules is but a poor reflection – and upside-down to boot!

The two constellations are similar in shape – you can see the outline of a man up there – but the stars are faint and undistinguished. Shame – because Hercules was one of the ancient Greeks' main legends, famous for his 12 labours of heroism.

Dig a little deeper, however, and you'll find a fascinating constellation. Outside the rectangular main 'body' of the hero, and to the south, you'll find **Rasalgethi** – Hercules' head. At 600 times the Sun's girth, this is one of the biggest stars known.

This distended object, close to the end of its life, flops and billows in its death throes. As a result, it varies in brightness, changing from third to fourth magnitude over a period of about 90 days.

Hercules boasts one of the most spectacular sights in the northern night sky. Go back to the 'rectangle' and look about a quarter of the way down from the top right-hand star (**eta Herculis** – a sun-like star), and you'll see a fuzzy patch. In a small telescope, **M13** – a globular cluster made of almost a million stars – looks like a swarm of bees.

▼ The sky at 11 pm in mid-May, with Moon positions at three-day intervals either side of Full Moon. The star positions are also correct for midnight at the beginning of

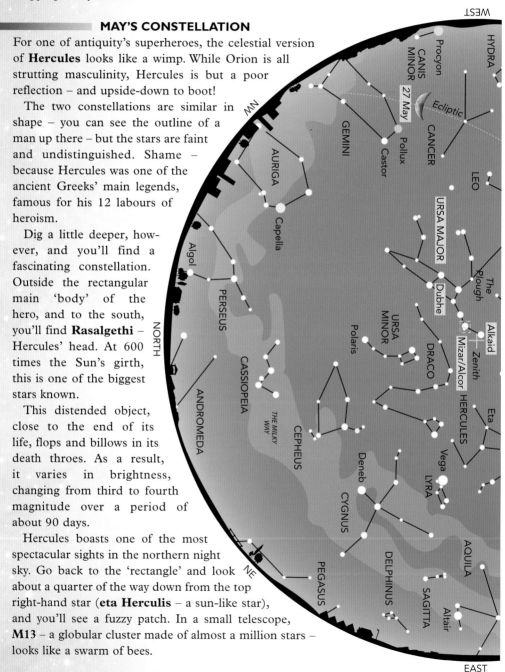

May, and 10 pm at the end of the month. The planets move slightly relative to the stars during the month.

PLANETS ON VIEW

During the first week of May, you'll find tiny **Mercury** very low in the north-west around 10 pm, close to the Pleiades. During this time its magnitude plummets from +1.2 to +2.5, as it drops down towards the Sun.

Saturn reigns supreme during the later evening. Nestling under the belly of Leo (the Lion), Saturn shines at magnitude +0.8, and sets around 3.20 am. Through a small telescope, check out its rings – currently seen almost edge-on – and the brightest of its 60 moons.

The planetary action is now hotting up in the dawn twilight. You can't miss **Venus**, blazing at magnitude −4.5 in the east, in Pisces. At the start of May, the Morning Star rises at 4.20 am, appearing ever earlier until it's above the horizon at 3.20 am by the month's end. Through a telescope, you'll see it change from a crescent to half-lit during May.

To the south-east, you'll find the second brightest planet, **Jupiter**, in Capricornus. At magnitude −2.3, it's only one-eighth as bright as Venus; to compensate, you can see Jupiter rather better as it is higher above the horizon glow, rising about an hour before Venus at the start of May, and as early as 1.30 am by month-end. It's very close to the star mu Capricorni between 18–24 May, which, at magnitude +5.1, is similar to Jupiter's brightest moon, Ganymede. A few days later, it passes Neptune (see Special Events).

WEST

CANCER

Regulus

The Sickle

3 May

HYDRA

Saturn

URSA MAJOR

LEO

CANES VENATICI

CORVUS

6 May

Spica

Ecliptic

CENTAURUS

SOUTH

BOÖTES

VIRGO

HYDRA

Mizar/Alcor
Zenith

Alkaid

Arcturus

SERPENS

9 May

LIBRA

eta Herculis

M13

CORONA BOREALIS

Gemma

Rasalgethi

OPHIUCHUS

SCORPIUS

Antares

HERCULES

AQUILA

THE MILKY WAY

SE

Altair

SERPENS

EAST

Saturn

Moon

	MOON	
Date	**Time**	**Phase**
1	9.44 pm	First Quarter
9	5.01 am	Full Moon
17	8.26 am	Last Quarter
24	1.11 pm	New Moon
31	4.22 am	First Quarter

Saturn

May's Objects
Mizar and
Alcor

Mars lies about 5 degrees to the left of Venus, but it is faint at only magnitude +1.2 – it becomes more easily seen as it rises higher in the sky at the end of May. **Uranus**, also in Pisces, is so faint (magnitude +5.9) it's difficult to spot in the dawn twilight.

Neptune (magnitude +7.9) lies very near to Jupiter; the two planets pass on 28 May (see Special Events).

MOON

The Moon lies near Leo's brightest star, Regulus, on 2 May, and passes Saturn between 3 and 4 May. It's near Spica, in Virgo, on 6 May. On the night of 10/11 May, the Moon rises in close proximity to Antares, the red giant star in Scorpius. In the early morning of 17 May, the First Quarter Moon lies next to giant planet Jupiter; and in the dawn of 21 May, the crescent Moon forms a lovely pair with Venus.

SPECIAL EVENTS

The maximum of the Eta Aquarid meteor shower falls on **4/5 May**, when tiny pieces of Halley's Comet burn up in Earth's atmosphere.

On the morning of **28 May**, Jupiter passes only a degree from Neptune – providing an ideal chance to spot the outermost planet. Through a small telescope, you'll see Jupiter's moons laid out left to right, from Callisto to Ganymede. Shift your view upwards (be careful of your direction if using an inverting telescope!) by twice the distance between Callisto and Ganymede, and look for a 'star' about one-tenth the brightness of Jupiter's moons: that's Neptune. This is the first of three conjunctions of these planets in 2009 – the others occur in July and December.

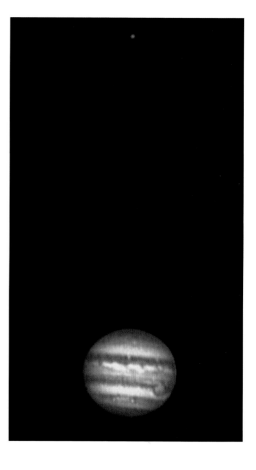

MAY'S OBJECT

Home in on the 'kink' in the tail of **Ursa Major** (the Great Bear), and you'll spot the most famous pair of stars in the sky – **Mizar** (magnitude +2.4) and **Alcor** (magnitude +4.0). Generations of astronomers have referred to them as 'the horse and rider', and students have been raised on the fact that the pair make up a classic double-star system, orbiting in each other's embrace. But *are* Mizar and Alcor an item? It seems not. Although they both lie about 80 light years away, they are separated by 3 light years – nearly the distance from the Sun to our

⊙ *Viewing tip*

For early birds, Venus is a real treat this month. The Morning Star is at its maximum brilliance (magnitude −4.5) at the beginning of May. If you have a small telescope, though, don't be too impatient to observe Venus. While the sky is dark, the cloud-wreathed planet appears so bright that it's difficult to make out anything on its disc. It's best to wait until the dawn sky has brightened and the other stars disappear. You can then see the globe of Venus appearing fainter against a pale blue sky. *But stop observing when the Sun rises, or you risk catching its blinding glare in your field of view.*

◄ *A combination of separate images made by James Jefferson from Ruislip shows the relative sizes of Jupiter and Neptune as they will appear on 27/28 May, though the separation will be over eight times that shown here. He used a Meade ETX 125 with an Atik 2C CCD camera, combining many separate video exposures for each object.*

closest star, Proxima Centauri. Undoubtedly, Mizar is a complex star system, having a companion visible through a telescope which is itself a double; in total, there are four stars involved. But it appears that Alcor is an innocent bystander. Although it shares its path through space with Mizar, the two are probably just members of the 'stellar association' that largely makes up Ursa Major. Unlike most constellations, the stars of the Great Bear are genuinely linked by birth (with the exceptions of **Dubhe** and **Alkaid**, at opposite ends of the central 'Plough').

MAY'S PICTURE

Two gas giants: **Jupiter**, the biggest planet in the Solar System, and **Neptune** (above) – our most distant world. Jupiter is a crazy planet. Large enough to contain all the other planets put together, it rotates in less than ten hours. This phenomenal spin-rate makes it bulge around its equator, and draws its clouds out into humbug-like bands. But Neptune, over 4,500 million kilometres away, still has tricks up its sleeve. It boasts the fastest winds in the Solar System – over 2000 km/h.

MAY'S TOPIC
Star Colours

Spring is well and truly here, with **Arcturus** gracing our night skies again. The fourth-brightest star in the sky, it follows the two bears around the heavens. In legend, Arcturus was 'the Bearkeeper' – responsible in particular for looking after Arcas, the Little Bear.

Look at the colour of Arcturus. It's orange-red: a sure sign that 'the Bearkeeper' is a cool star. Its surface temperature is just 4000°C, as compared to 5500°C for our yellow Sun.

Star colours are a good guide to their temperatures. The hottest stars are blue-white. White stars come next, then yellow, orange and red.

Arcturus is a red giant: a distended star close to the end of its life. Its atmosphere has expanded, and cooled. But it's no match for **Antares** in Scorpius, which is just rising in the south-east. This bloated, baleful red star got its name from 'Anti Ares' – the rival of Mars.

Antares is 700 times the size of our Sun. If placed in the Solar System, it would stretch all the way to the asteroid belt. Now – in its death throes – the star's temperature has dropped to a mere 3200°C.

Contrast this with **Spica**, the bright, conspicuously blue-white star at the heart of Virgo. This is a star in the prime of life. Spica boasts a surface temperature of 22,000°C, and is more than 2000 times brighter than the Sun.

On 21 June, the Sun hits the Summer Solstice – the date when our local star reaches its highest position over the northern hemisphere. This has been celebrated as a seasonal ritual for millennia, leading to the construction of massive stone monuments aligned on the rising Sun at midsummer. Undeniably, our ancestors had formidable astronomical knowledge.

As a result of the Solstice, we experience long days, and short nights – not the best time to do astronomy! But if the summer nights are balmy, it's a glorious time to go out and experience the heavens – watching the whole sky, and seeing the season's emerging constellations such as **Hercules, Lyra, Cygnus** and **Aquila**.

JUNE'S CONSTELLATION

Libra (the Scales) – this faint quadrilateral of stars lies close to the constellation of **Scorpius**, and the Greeks actually regarded it as part of the celestial crustacean. They deemed its three brightest stars as being the claws of the scorpion.

The Arabs gave these stars delightful names. Alpha Librae – although boasting a magnitude of just +2.8 – is called **Zubenelgenubi**, meaning 'the southern claw'. It is 77 light years away, and has a faint companion of magnitude +5.2, which is visible in good binoculars or a small telescope.

The faintest of the three stars is **Zubenelakrab** ('the scorpion's claw'), which is 152 light years distant. It shines at a magnitude of +3.9.

But the brightest star in the constellation is beta Librae – **Zubeneschamali** ('the northern claw'). It has a fascinating history: 160 light years away, it now shines at a brightness of magnitude +2.6 (confusingly, brighter than alpha Librae!). Rumour has it that at least two of the Greek astronomer-philosophers of 2000 years ago rated it as brilliant

▼ The sky at 11 pm in mid-June, with Moon positions at three-day intervals either side of Full Moon. The star positions are also correct for midnight at the beginning of

WEST

25 June
Regulus
Ecliptic
The Sickle
CANCER
LEO
CANES VENATICI
Pollux
Castor
GEMINI
URSA MAJOR
The Plough
AURIGA
HERCULES
Capella
Zenith
NORTH
Polaris
URSA MINOR
DRACO
Vega
CASSIOPEIA
CEPHEUS
LYRA
PERSEUS
Algol
THE MILKY WAY
Deneb
CYGNUS
ANDROMEDA
DELPHINUS
NE
Square of Pegasus
PEGASUS

EAST

June, and 10 pm at the end of the month. The planets move slightly relative to the stars during the month.

as red Antares – the first-magnitude star that marks the scorpion's heart.

Might this blue dwarf star have flared up in the past? There are suspicions of a companion star, which could have dumped material on beta Librae in recorded history. In which case – watch that star in case it happens again!

Finally: something you won't be able to see in Libra. It boasts a faint star named Gliese 581, which appears to be surrounded by three planets. From the gravitational 'wobbles' on the star, one of them seems to be of relatively low mass – five times heavier than the Earth – and lives within its star's 'habitable zone', where life could be possible. But researchers aren't optimistic, believing that the parent star's heating effect on the planet's atmosphere will have led to a run-away 'greenhouse effect'.

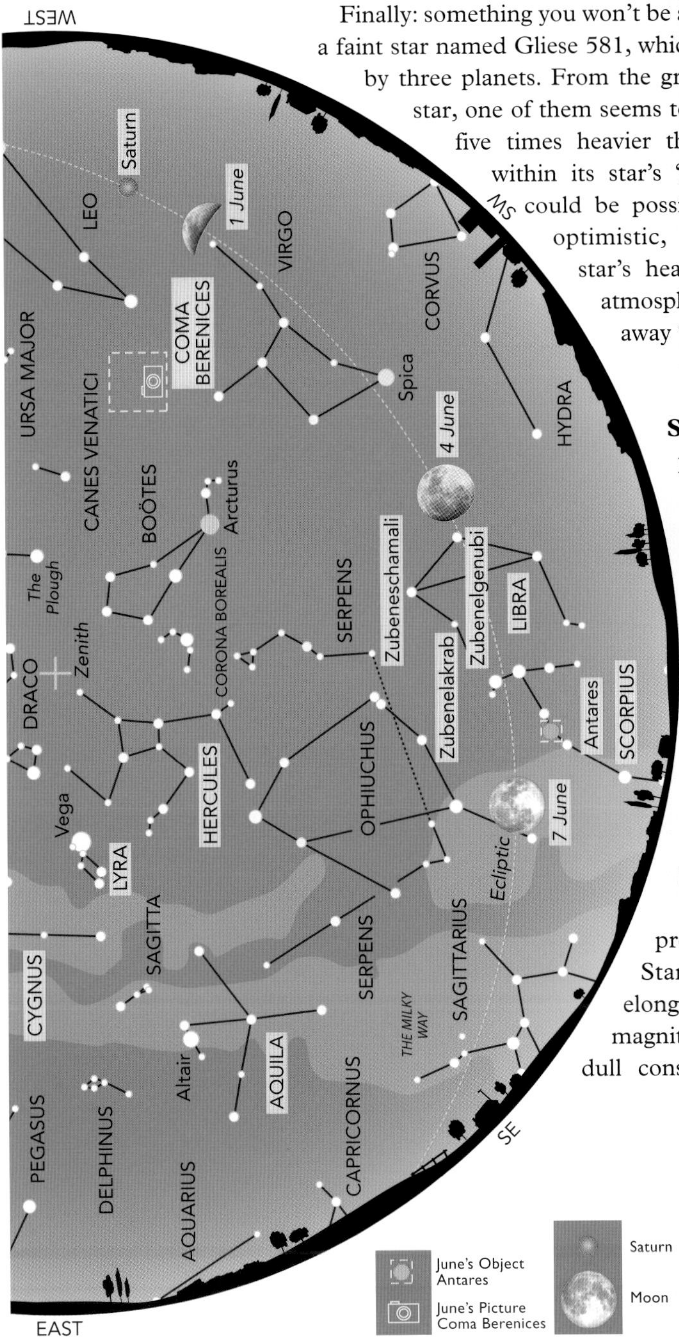
WEST
SW
SOUTH
SE
EAST
Saturn
1 June
4 June
7 June
LEO
VIRGO
CORVUS
COMA BERENICES
URSA MAJOR
CANES VENATICI
Spica
HYDRA
BOÖTES
Arcturus
The Plough
CORONA BOREALIS
SERPENS
Zubeneschamali
Zubenelgenubi
LIBRA
Zenith
DRACO
Zubenelakrab
Antares
SCORPIUS
HERCULES
OPHIUCHUS
Vega
LYRA
Ecliptic
SAGITTA
SAGITTARIUS
CYGNUS
SERPENS
THE MILKY WAY
Altair
AQUILA
CAPRICORNUS
PEGASUS
DELPHINUS
AQUARIUS
June's Object
Antares
June's Picture
Coma Berenices
Saturn
Moon

PLANETS ON VIEW

Saturn is the sole planetary presence in the evening sky, shining at magnitude +1.0, below Leo. Through a telescope, its rings look very thin as we approach edge-on viewing in September.

Giant planet **Jupiter** is now hoving into view around 0.30 am, between Capricornus and Aquarius. At magnitude −2.6, it is by far the brightest object in that barren region of sky.

Venus is queen of the pre-dawn sky. The Morning Star reaches greatest western elongation on 5 June, shining at magnitude −4.2 in the otherwise dull constellation of Pisces. At the

MOON		
Date	**Time**	**Phase**
7	7.12 pm	Full Moon
15	11.14 pm	Last Quarter
22	8.35 pm	New Moon
29	12.28 pm	First Quarter

beginning of June, Venus is rising in the east at about 3.20 am; by the end of the month, it's in Aries and you'll see it as early as 2.30 am, as it approaches the Pleiades. On 21 and 22 June, Venus is near Mars (see Special Events).

Red Planet **Mars** is also making its presence felt in the early morning, in Aries, though it's still comparatively dim (magnitude +1.1) in a sky that's never totally dark at this time of the year in parts of the country. It's rising at 3.20 am at the beginning of June, and 2.00 am at the end of the month. Venus passes nearby on the mornings of 21 and 22 June (see Special Events).

Uranus, in Pisces at magnitude +5.9, rises around 1.30 am. **Neptune** (magnitude +7.9), in Capricornus, rises around 0.30 am – and lies within a degree of Jupiter all month.

Mercury is technically a morning star, reaching greatest western elongation on 13 June, but it is too low in the twilight to be easily seen.

MOON

The Moon lies near Spica, in Virgo, on 2 June; and it's very close to Scorpius's brightest star, Antares, on the morning of 7 June. On the nights of 12/13 and 13/14 June, the Moon is near Jupiter. In the early morning of 19 June, the crescent Moon lies above Venus and much fainter Mars; and the following morning, it is to the left of these two planets. Back in the evening sky, the crescent Moon is near Regulus on 26 June, Saturn on 27 June and Spica again on 30 June.

SPECIAL EVENTS

21 June, 6.45 am: Summer Solstice. The Sun reaches its most northerly point in the sky, so 21 June is Midsummer's Day, with the longest period of daylight. Correspondingly, we have the shortest nights.

Brilliant Venus speeds under Mars in the wee small hours, during the second half of June. They are closest on the mornings of **21** and **22 June**, when Mars lies two degrees above Venus, shining only one-hundredth as brightly.

JUNE'S OBJECT

Its name means 'the rival of Mars' – and you can see why. Look low in the south this month for a baleful red star that marks the heart of the constellation of Scorpius. At 600 light years away, **Antares** is a bloated red giant star near the end of its life. Running out of its central supplies of nuclear fuel, its core has

▲ The Coma Berenices star cluster is visible with the naked eye on a good night, occupying a considerable part of the constellation. This view was made by Robin Scagell using a Canon A-1 camera through a 135 mm f/2.8 telephoto lens. He gave a six-minute exposure on Ektachrome 1600 film.

shrunk and heated up, causing its outer layers to billow out and cool. Now Antares is 700 times bigger than our Sun, 10,000 times more luminous, and at least 15 times heavier. Placed at the centre of our Solar System, it would engulf all the planets out to Mars. And its size isn't constant. Antares' gravity hasn't got to grips with its extended girth, making the star swell and shrink – changing in brightness as it does so. The giant star has a small blue companion (magnitude +5.0), which is hard to see against Antares' glare. Just visible in a small telescope, the star circles the red giant every 878 years. Eventually, Antares's core will collapse completely, and it will explode as a brilliant supernova.

JUNE'S PICTURE

The constellation of **Coma Berenices** is home to two clusters: one, a giant conurbation of galaxies and – here – a beautiful star cluster. The constellation is charmingly named after the hair of Queen Berenice, wife of the Egyptian Ptolemy III. She pledged her beauteous locks to the heavens if her husband returned safe from battle. Berenice's star cluster is spread over an area ten times larger than the disc of the Full Moon. It's a great sight through binoculars.

JUNE'S TOPIC
Constellations

Libra, our constellation of the month, highlights humankind's obsession to 'join up the dots' in the sky, and weave stories around them – even if the shape of the star pattern bears little relation to its name.

But why? One is that the constellations on view change during the year as the Earth moves around the Sun, and the constellations acted as an '*aide memoire*' to where we are in our annual cycle – something of particular use to the ancient farming communities.

Another is that the stars were a great steer to navigation at sea. In fact, scholars believe that the Greek astronomers 'mapped' their legends on to the sky specifically so that sailors crossing the Mediterranean would associate certain constellations essential to navigation with their traditional stories.

But not all the world saw the sky through western eyes. The Chinese divided up the sky into a plethora of tiny constellations – with only three or four stars apiece. And the Australian Aborigines, in their dark deserts, were so overwhelmed with stars that they made constellations out of the dark places where they couldn't see any stars!

This month, we continue the International Year of Astronomy with a focus on a little-known English astronomer – Thomas Harriot. The Oxford-educated scholar lived in the grounds of Syon House in west London, and – on 26 July 1609 – he observed and sketched the Moon through his telescope, several months before Galileo. Harriot's ground-breaking observations will be celebrated with an anniversary at Syon Park on Sunday, 26 July 2009.

JULY'S CONSTELLATION

Low down in the south, you'll find a constellation that's shaped rather like a teapot. The handle lies to the left, and the spout to the right!

To the ancient Greeks, the star pattern of **Sagittarius** represented an archer, with the torso of a man and the body of a horse. The 'handle' of the teapot represents his upper body, the curve of three stars to the right is his bent bow, while the end of the spout is the point of the arrow, aimed at **Scorpius**, the fearsome celestial scorpion.

Sagittarius is rich with nebulae and star clusters. If you have a clear night (and preferably from a southern latitude), sweep Sagittarius with binoculars for some fantastic sights. Above the spout lies the wonderful **Lagoon Nebula** – visible to the naked eye on clear nights. This is a region where stars are being born. Between the teapot and the neighbouring constellation, Aquila, you'll find a bright patch of stars in the Milky Way, catalogued as **M24**. Raise your binoculars higher to spot another star-forming region, the **Omega Nebula**.

Finally, on a very dark night you may spot a fuzzy patch, above and to the left of the teapot's lid. This is the globular cluster **M22** – a swarm of almost a million stars that lies 10,000 light years away.

▼ The sky at 11 pm in mid-July, with Moon positions at three-day intervals either side of Full Moon. The star positions are also correct for midnight at the beginning of

WEST

VIRGO

LEO

CANES VENATICI

The Plough

BOÖTES

The Sickle

URSA MAJOR

URSA MINOR

Polaris

DRACO

HERCULES

Zenith

AURIGA

Capella

NORTH

CASSIOPEIA

CEPHEUS

THE MILKY WAY

Deneb

CYGNUS

PERSEUS

Algol

TRIANGULUM

ANDROMEDA

PEGASUS

Square of Pegasus

PISCES

NE

EAST

WEST

July, and 10 pm at the end of the month. The planets move slightly relative to the stars during the month.

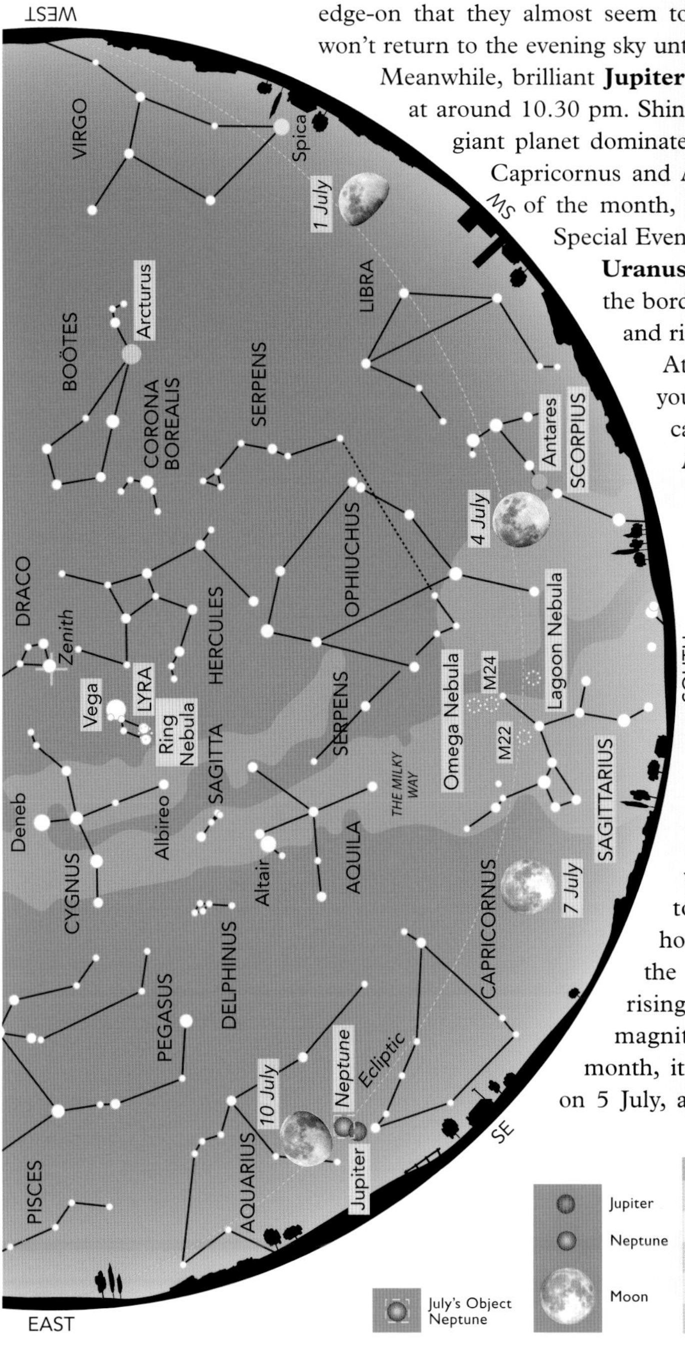

PLANETS ON VIEW

Saturn (magnitude +1.1), under the hindquarters of Leo, is hanging on in the west in the evening sky, though it's sinking into the twilight glow. At the beginning of July, Saturn is setting at about 0.15 am, while at the end of the month it's gone by 10.20 pm. Through a telescope, we see its rings so close to edge-on that they almost seem to have disappeared. Saturn won't return to the evening sky until the very end of the year.

Meanwhile, brilliant **Jupiter** is rising in the south-east, at around 10.30 pm. Shining at magnitude −2.8, the giant planet dominates the dull constellations of Capricornus and Aquarius. For the first half of the month, it's close to **Neptune** (see Special Events).

Uranus (magnitude +5.8) lies on the borders of Aquarius and Pisces, and rises at about 11.30 pm.

At the beginning of July, you'll find Venus and Mars canoodling together between Aries and Taurus, and rising around 2.30 am. During the month, **Mars** moves gradually higher in the sky, until by the end of the month it rises as early as 1 am. The Red Planet, at magnitude +1.1, lies in Taurus and it passes under the Pleiades on 12 July.

Venus, also in Taurus all month, parts company with Mars and heads back towards the north-eastern horizon. By the end of July, the brilliant Morning Star is rising at 2.15 am, blazing at magnitude −4.0. During the month, it passes below the Pleiades on 5 July, and then skims the Hyades

MOON

Date	Time	Phase
7	10.21 am	Full Moon
15	10.53 am	Last Quarter
22	3.34 am	New Moon
28	11.00 pm	First Quarter

Jupiter
Neptune
Moon
July's Object Neptune

WEST

EAST

31

star cluster and the Crab Nebula (see Special Events). **Mercury** lies too close to the Sun to be seen this month.

MOON

On 10 July, the Moon is near Jupiter – just when the giant planet has its closest approach to Neptune (see Special Events). In the early hours of 18 July, the crescent Moon occults some of the stars in the Pleiades around 2 am, just as the sky is brightening, with Mars below. And the morning of 19 July sees the narrow Moon immediately above Venus. Returning to the evening sky, the Moon lies near Spica on 27 July, and Antares on 31 July.

SPECIAL EVENTS

On **4 July**, the Earth is at aphelion, its furthest point from the Sun.

Jupiter passes less than a degree below Neptune on **10 July**. But be careful: there's also a star involved! Above Jupiter, you'll find mu Capricorni (magnitude +5.1), about the same brightness as Jupiter's moons. The same distance above again lies Neptune, some ten times fainter at magnitude +7.9. And the Moon lies only 3 degrees away. This is the second of three conjunctions of Jupiter and Neptune this year (see also May and December).

Venus moves through the upper edge of the Hyades star cluster on the morning of **13 July**, passing 3 degrees from Aldebaran. And on the morning of **27 July**, Venus is just half a degree below the Crab Nebula, the faint remains (magnitude +8.4) of a supernova seen in 1054. You'll need a good telescope and a clear horizon to the north-east to see this interesting event before the sky brightens.

There's a total eclipse of the Sun on **22 July**, though it's not visible from Britain. The track of totality passes from India, through Burma (Myanmar) and China, to end in the Pacific. As seen from Shanghai, the total eclipse will last almost 6 minutes. A partial eclipse is visible from south-east and eastern Asia, and most of Indonesia.

26 July sees celebrations in Syon Park, west London, commemorating Thomas Harriot's use of the telescope (see page 30).

JULY'S OBJECT

With Pluto being demoted to the status of being a mere 'ice dwarf', **Neptune** is officially the most remote planet in our Solar System. It lies 4,500 billion kilometres away from the Sun – 30 times the Earth's distance – in the twilight zone of our family of worlds. The gas giant takes nearly 165 years to circle the Sun.

This month, it's just visible through a small telescope low in Capricornus. But you need a space-probe to get up close and

▶ *A composite image of the total solar eclipse of 29 March 2006, photographed from Side in Turkey by Nick King. He used a Canon 300D digital camera with a 100–400 mm Canon lens and 2x tele-extender to combine a range of exposures in order to capture both detail in the corona and Earthshine on the Moon.*

◉ *Viewing tip*

This is the month when you really need a good, unobstructed view to the southern horizon, to make out the summer constellations of Scorpius and Sagittarius. They never rise high in temperate latitudes, so make the best of a southerly view – especially over the sea – if you're away on holiday. A good southern horizon is also best for views of the planets, because they rise highest when they are in the south.

personal to the planet. In 1989, Voyager 2 managed this. It discovered a turquoise world 17 times more massive than Earth, cloaked in hydrogen and helium.

Neptune has a family of 13 moons – one of which, Triton, boasts erupting ice volcanoes. And, like the other outer worlds, it's encircled by rings of debris – although, in Neptune's case, they're very faint.

For a planet so far from the Sun, Neptune is amazingly frisky. Its core blazes at 7000°C – hotter than the surface of the Sun. This internal heat drives dramatic storms, and winds of 2000 km/h – the fastest in the Solar System.

JULY'S PICTURE

Those lucky enough to be in China and the southern Pacific on 22 July will be treated to a total eclipse of the Sun. In this sensational image, the Sun's outer atmosphere – the corona – flashes into view behind the dark disc of the Moon. Nothing prepares you for a total eclipse. The Sun disappears – and it turns into a truly frightening Chinese dragon-mask.

JULY'S TOPIC
Nebulae

We think of the stars as being constant and unchanging, but a long, leisurely look at the summer sky proves anything but. Sweep Sagittarius with binoculars, and you'll find it studded with nebulae – gas clouds which are the nurseries of new stars. These fledgling stars grow up to make hot young stars like **Vega**, shining as a result of nuclear reactions in their searingly-hot cores. As stars age – and their hydrogen fuel starts to run out – they develop the problems of middle age. Look no further than orange **Arcturus** and baleful red **Antares** (in Scorpius) for stars that have swollen up and cooled down near the end of their lives. Stars like these will eventually puff off their distended atmospheres into space, leaving a brief-lived 'planetary nebula' (like the **Ring Nebula** in Lyra), surrounding the now-defunct core. The nebula will soon disperse, leaving the cooling core – a white dwarf – alone in space, destined to become a cold, black cinder.

We have the Glorious Twelfth for astronomers this month: 12–13 August is the maximum of the **Perseid** meteor shower. This is the year's most reliable display of shooting stars, and it also conveniently takes place during the summer, when it's not too uncomfortable to stay up late under the stars!

Every August, the Earth runs into fragments of dust from Comet Swift-Tuttle. The comet dust impacts our atmosphere at 210,000 km/h and burns up in a streak of light. Because of perspective, the meteors all seem to diverge from the same part of the sky – the meteor *radiant* – which lies in the constellation Perseus.

AUGUST'S CONSTELLATION

Draco (the Dragon) – this cosmic beast writhes between the two bears in the northern sky. Like Hydra (see April), Draco is probably another constellation associated with Hercules' 12 labours, because its head rests on the (upside-down) superhero's feet. In this case, Hercules had to get past a crowd of nymphs and slay a 100-headed dragon (called Ladon) before his task – which, in this case, was stealing the immortal golden apples from the gardens of the Hesperides.

Confusingly, the brightest star in Draco is gamma Draconis – which ought to be third in the pecking order. Orange **Eltanin** shines at magnitude +2.2, and lies 148 light years away. But all this is to change. In 1.5 million years, it will swing past the Earth at a distance of 28 light years, outshining even Sirius.

Alpha Draconis – which, by rights, should be the brightest in the constellation – stumbles in at a mere magnitude of +3.7. **Thuban** lies just below Ursa Minor, in the tail of the dragon.

But what Thuban lacks in brightness, it makes up for in fame: 300 light years away, Thuban was our Pole Star in the years around 2800 BC. It actually lay closer to the celestial pole

▼ The sky at 11 pm in mid-August, with Moon positions at three-day intervals either side of Full Moon. The star positions are also correct for midnight

at the beginning of August, and 10 pm at the end of the month. The planets move slightly relative to the stars during the month.

than Polaris does now – just 2.5 arcminutes, as opposed to 42 for Polaris.

The swinging of Earth's axis – like the toppling of a spinning top – takes place over a period of 26,000 years. 'Precession' means that, over the millennia, the Earth's North Pole points to a number of stars while we spin underneath – so they appear stationary in the sky. Look forward to AD 14,000, when brilliant **Vega** will take over the pole!

PLANETS ON VIEW

August belongs to **Jupiter**. It's opposite the Sun in the sky, at its brightest – and at its closest point to the Earth this year – on 14 August. At magnitude −2.9, the giant planet is by far the most brilliant object in the dim constellation Capricornus, and this month Jupiter is shining low in the south all night long. Through binoculars or a small telescope, watch the endless dance of its four biggest moons – on 1 to 5 August, they are joined by the star 45 Capricorni (see Special Events).

Neptune lies in Capricornus, too. Just 3 degrees to the left of Jupiter, it is also above the horizon all night long. But, at magnitude +7.8, you'll need a telescope to find it. The most distant planet is at opposition on 17 August.

The penultimate planet, **Uranus** (magnitude +5.8), lies on the borders of Aquarius and Pisces. It is also visible all night.

Mars is rising in the north-east around 1.00 am at the beginning of

WEST

CORONA BOREALIS

LIBRA

SERPENS

SCORPIUS

DRACO

Eltanin

Vega

M13

HERCULES

OPHIUCHUS

Zenith

LYRA

SAGITTA

SERPENS

THE MILKY WAY

AQUILA

Altair

SAGITTARIUS

3 Aug

SOUTH

Deneb

CYGNUS

SUMMER TRIANGLE

DELPHINUS

Neptune

Jupiter

CAPRICORNUS

ANDROMEDA

PEGASUS

6 Aug

PISCIS AUSTRINUS

Square of Pegasus

AQUARIUS

Uranus

9 Aug

Ecliptic

PISCES

CETUS

SE

EAST

			MOON		
○	Jupiter				
○	Uranus	**Date**	**Time**	**Phase**	
○	Neptune	6	1.55 am	Full Moon	
		13	7.55 pm	Last Quarter	
●	Moon	20	11.01 am	New Moon	
		27	12.42 pm	First Quarter	

August's Object
Delta Cephei

August's Picture
M13

Radiant of
Perseids

35

August, and 0.20 am by the end of the month. Shining at magnitude +1.0 between the horns of Taurus (the Bull), the Red Planet is a close match in brightness to the constellation's main star, the red giant Aldebaran. Mid-month it passes the Crab Nebula (see Special Events).

As the Morning Star, **Venus** starts the month rising earlier than at any other time this year (2.20 am) – over 3 hours before the Sun. By the end of August, you'll have to wait until 3.10 am. At magnitude −4.0, Venus dominates the constellations of Taurus and Gemini.

Mercury and **Saturn** are too close to the Sun to be seen this month.

MOON

On the evening of 6 August, the Full Moon passes just above Jupiter, and then – in the early hours of the following morning – Neptune. Early in the morning of 16 August, the Moon lies near Mars. And just before dawn on 18 August, you'll see the narrow crescent Moon forming a charming pair with Venus. Back in the evening sky, the Moon lies close to Antares on 27 August.

SPECIAL EVENTS

During the first week of August, Jupiter's family of four moons is joined by an interloper of roughly the same brightness, the star 45 Capricorni (magnitude +6.0). If you have a telescope, look out for a rare event on **3/4 August**, when Jupiter moves right in front of the star: the occultation starts at 11 pm and ends at 0.45 am.

The maximum of the annual **Perseid** meteor shower falls on **12/13 August**. You'll see Perseid meteors for several nights around the time of maximum.

There's a treat for deep-space watchers in the early hours of **16** and **17 August**, when Mars passes above the Crab Nebula, at a separation of just over a degree.

AUGUST'S OBJECT

At first glance, the star **Delta Cephei**, in the constellation representing King Cepheus, doesn't seem to merit any special attention. It's a yellowish star of magnitude +4 – easily visible to the naked eye, but not prominent. A telescope reveals a companion star. But this star holds the key to the size of the Universe.

Carefully check the brightness of this star over days and weeks, and you'll see that it changes regularly, from +3.6 (brightest) to +4.3 (faintest), every 5 days 9 hours. It's a result

⊙ *Viewing tip*
Have a Perseids party! You don't need any optical equipment – in fact, telescopes and binoculars will restrict your view of the meteor shower. The ideal viewing equipment is your unaided eye, plus a sleeping bag and a lounger on the lawn. If you want to make measurements, a stopwatch and clock are good for timings, while a piece of string will help to measure the length of the meteor trail.

of the star literally swelling and shrinking in size, from 32 to 35 times the Sun's diameter.

Astronomers have found that stars like this – Cepheid variables – show a link between their period of variation and their intrinsic luminosity. By observing the star's period and brightness as it appears in the sky, astronomers can work out a Cepheid's distance. With the Hubble Space Telescope, astronomers have now measured Cepheids in the Virgo cluster of galaxies, which lies 55 million light years away.

AUGUST'S PICTURE

The globular cluster **M13** is just visible to the unaided eye in Hercules. Made up of hundreds of thousands of old red stars, it is one of the most ancient objects in our Galaxy. M13 is part of a swarm of globular clusters that surround the Milky Way. In 1974, astronomers at the Arecibo Observatory in Puerto Rico beamed a message to M13 from their giant radio telescope, telling of life on Planet Earth – it will take 25,000 years to arrive.

▲ *Eddie Guscott photographed the globular cluster M13 from Corringham in Essex with a TMB 130 mm refractor. He used a total of 4 hours' exposure time through separate filters to make the image.*

AUGUST'S TOPIC
Centre of the Milky Way

The Milky Way stretches all the way around our sky, as a gently glowing band. In reality, it is a spiral shape of some 200 billion stars, with the Sun about halfway out. The centre of the Milky Way lies in the direction of the constellation Sagittarius. But our view of the galactic centre is obscured by great clouds of dark dust that block the view for even the most powerful telescopes.

Now, however, instruments observing at other wavelengths have lifted the veil on the Galaxy's heart. Infrared telescopes can see the heat radiation from stars and gas clouds at the galactic centre. These objects are speeding around so fast that they must be in the grip of something with fantastically strong gravity. In 2002, astronomers at the European Southern Observatory in Chile discovered a star that is orbiting the Galaxy's centre at over 18 million km/h! In the meantime, radio astronomers have found that the Galaxy's exact heart is marked by a tiny source of radiation: Sagittarius A*.

Putting all these observations together, astronomers have concluded that the core of the Milky Way must contain a heavyweight black hole. The latest data from 2008 indicate that it is as massive as 4 million Suns. When a speeding star comes too close to this invisible monster, it is ripped apart. There's a final shriek from the star's gases – producing the observed radio waves – before they fall into the black hole, and disappear from our Universe.

Autumn is here – with its unsettled weather – and we have the star patterns to match. **Aquarius** (hardly one of the most spectacular constellations) is part of a group of 'watery' star patterns which include **Cetus** (the Sea Monster), **Capricornus** (the Sea Goat), **Pisces** (the Fishes), **Piscis Austrinus** (the Southern Fish) and **Delphinus** (the Dolphin). With the exception of beautiful Delphinus, they are all fairly barren constellations. There's speculation that the ancient Babylonians associated this region with water because the Sun passed through this zone of the heavens during the rainy season, from February to March. They saw Aquarius as a man (the Water Carrier), pouring a water jug, marked by the faint central four stars of the constellation.

SEPTEMBER'S CONSTELLATION

Capricornus (the Sea Goat) – as noted above, this is one of a group of wet and watery constellations that swim in the celestial sea below **Pegasus** (the Winged Horse). But Capricornus had a special significance for ancient peoples. Over 2500 years ago, the Sun nestled amongst its stars at the time of the Winter Solstice. It showed to them that the year was about to turn around: the hours of darkness were at an end, and life-giving spring was on the way. So this obscure triangle of faint stars may have been one of humanity's first constellations.

Algedi is the most interesting star in the constellation, lying at top right. Even with the unaided eye, you can see that the star is double. The pair are faint (magnitudes +3.6 and +4.6 respectively) and they are not related. But each star is genuinely double, although you'll need a telescope to check this out.

By coincidence, the next-door star **Dabih** is also a double. The main member of this duo is a yellow star of magnitude +3.1;

▼ The sky at 11 pm in mid-September, with Moon positions at three-day intervals either side of Full Moon. The star positions are also correct for midnight at

WEST

OPHIUCHUS
SERPENS
CORONA BOREALIS
Arcturus
BOÖTES
CANES VENATICI
HERCULES
The Plough
DRACO
Vega
LYRA
CYGNUS
Deneb
CEPHEUS
Zenith
URSA MAJOR
URSA MINOR
Polaris
CASSIOPEIA
Double Cluster
ANDROMEDA
TRIANGULUM
ARIES
Capella
PERSEUS
Algol
Pleiades
AURIGA
THE MILKY WAY
10 Sept
Ecliptic
Aldebaran
TAURUS
NORTH
NW
NE

EAST

the beginning of September, and 10 pm at the end of the month. The planets move slightly relative to the stars during the month.

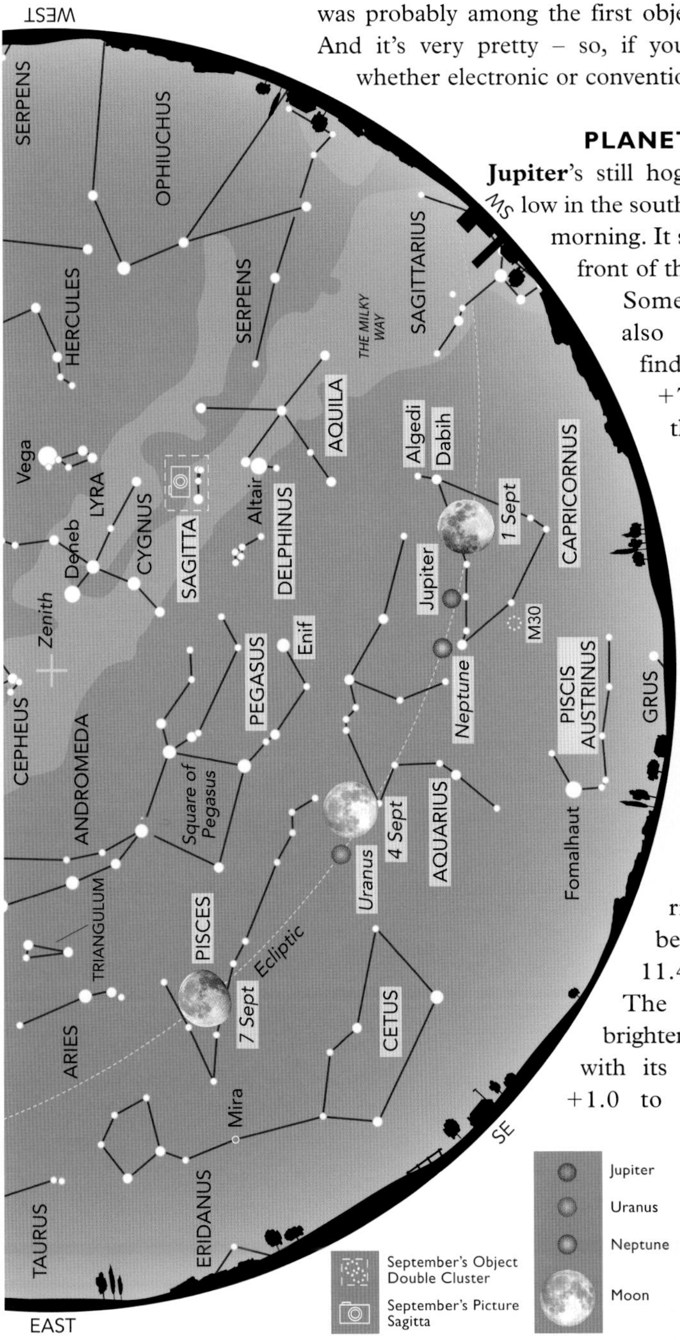

binoculars or a small telescope will reveal a blue companion at magnitude +6.0.

A telescope is also essential for the next beast in Capricornus – the globular cluster **M30**. The 7th-magnitude object, about 26,000 light years away, is just to the lower left of the constellation. This rather ragged ball of thousands of stars was probably among the first objects to form in our Galaxy. And it's very pretty – so, if you're into astrophotography, whether electronic or conventional – point and shoot!

PLANETS ON VIEW

Jupiter's still hogging the limelight, blazing low in the south until the small hours of the morning. It shines at magnitude −2.7 in front of the stars of Capricornus.

Some 5 degrees to the left, also in Capricornus, you will find **Neptune**. At magnitude +7.8, it's 15,000 times fainter than Jupiter, and requires a telescope.

Its twin planet, **Uranus** (at magnitude +5.7), is currently right on the borders of Aquarius and Pisces, and is visible in binoculars. It comes to opposition on 17 September, when it is due south at midnight and at its closest to the Earth this year.

Mars is creeping upwards in the early morning sky: rising at 0.20 am at the beginning of September, and 11.45 pm by month's end. The Red Planet is gradually brightening as the Earth approaches, with its magnitude changing from +1.0 to +0.8 during September.

September's Object
Double Cluster

September's Picture
Sagitta

	MOON		
	Date	Time	Phase
	4	5.02 pm	Full Moon
	12	3.16 am	Last Quarter
	18	7.44 pm	New Moon
	26	5.50 am	First Quarter

Jupiter
Uranus
Neptune
Moon

Moving through Gemini, it's near Castor and Pollux by the close of the month.

Brilliant **Venus** appears as the Morning Star, rising in the east around 3.10 am at the start of September, and 4.30 am at the end of the month. Venus shines at magnitude −4.0 among the stars of Cancer; and later in the month, Leo.

Saturn and **Mercury** are lost in the Sun's glare this month.

MOON

On 2 September, the Moon passes Jupiter. In the early morning of 5 September, it lies near Uranus. In the morning sky, the Moon lies near Mars on the mornings of 13 and 14 September, and close to Venus on 16 and 17 September – on the latter date, with Regulus lying between them. On the evening of 29 September, the Moon is back consorting with Jupiter

SPECIAL EVENTS

On the morning of **2 September**, Venus passes through the southern fringes of Praesepe, the Beehive star cluster. On 20 September, it passes less than a degree from Regulus.

It's the Autumn Equinox at 10.18 pm on **22 September**. The Sun is over the Equator as it heads southwards in the sky, and day and night are equal.

On **29 September**, NASA's Messenger spacecraft makes its third flyby of Mercury, sending it on a trajectory that will put Messenger into orbit around the innermost planet in March 2011.

◉ *Viewing tip*

Try to observe your favourite objects when they're well clear of the horizon. When you look low down, you're seeing through a large thickness of the atmosphere – which is always shifting and turbulent. It's like trying to observe the outside world from the bottom of a swimming pool! This turbulence makes the stars appear to twinkle. Low-down planets also twinkle – although to a lesser extent because they subtend tiny discs, and aren't so affected.

SEPTEMBER'S OBJECT

Two objects this time: the glorious **Double Cluster** in **Perseus**. These near-twin clusters of young stars – each covering an area bigger than the Full Moon – are visible to the unaided eye and are a gorgeous sight in binoculars. They're loaded with pretty young blue stars, and are both around 7000 light years away. Known as h and chi Persei, h is the older cluster at 5.6 million years, while chi is a mere 3.2 million years old. Each contains around 200 stars, and are part of what is known as the Perseus OB1 Association – a loose group of bright, hot stars that were born at roughly the same time. Associations and star clusters are important to researchers. They allow astronomers to monitor stars that are the same age – but have different masses – and the comparison helps researchers understand how stars evolve.

SEPTEMBER'S PICTURE

Look to the top right to see an upside-down coathanger in the stars! The main stars in this image are those of **Sagitta**. Many cultures – including the Greeks, Romans, Persians and Hebrews – saw it as an arrow. Legend has it that Sagitta was the weapon that Hercules used the kill the eagle **Aquila** (which lies just below Sagitta in the sky), because the bird delighted on nibbling the liver of the Titan Prometheus.

◄ The constellation of Sagitta is an ancient one, despite its small size. At far right is the interesting asterism known as the Coathanger, in Vulpecula. This photo was taken by Robin Scagell from Flackwell Heath, Buckinghamshire, using a Canon 10D camera with 100 mm telephoto lens. He combined three separate two-minute exposures and used a diffusion filter to enhance the star colours.

SEPTEMBER'S TOPIC
The Harvest Moon

It's the time of year when farmers work late into the night, bringing home their ripe crops before autumn sets in. And traditionally they are aided by the light of the 'Harvest Moon' – a huge glowing Full Moon that seems to hang constant in the evening sky, rising at the same time night after night. At first sight, that doesn't seem possible. After all, the Moon is moving around the Earth, once in just under a month, so it ought to rise roughly one hour later every night. But things in the sky are hardly ever that simple....

The Moon follows a tilted path around the sky (close to the line of the Ecliptic, which is marked on the star chart). And this path changes its angle with the horizon at different times of year. On September evenings, the Moon's path runs roughly parallel to the horizon, so night after night the Moon moves to the left in the sky, but it hardly moves downwards. The consequence is that the Moon rises around the same time for several consecutive nights. This year, Full Moon on 4 September rises at 7.17 pm (ideal for harvesting) – it rises just 13 minutes earlier the evening before, and 14 minutes later the night after.

This month the International Year of Astronomy celebrates the Moon again, and also the dazzling planet **Jupiter** (see Special Events). A glimpse of this supergiant world through a telescope is an unforgettable experience. Its rapid spin flattens the planet into an oval, making it look like a tangerine. And Jupiter's gas clouds are whipped up into horizontal bands of frenzy, giving the world the appearance of a cosmic humbug.

▼ The sky at 11 pm in mid-October, with Moon positions at three-day intervals either side of Full Moon. The star positions are also correct for midnight at

OCTOBER'S CONSTELLATION

It takes considerable imagination to see the line of stars making up **Andromeda** as a young princess chained to a rock, about to be gobbled up by a vast sea monster (**Cetus**) – but that's ancient legends for you. Despite its rather mundane appearance, the constellation contains some surprising delights. One is **Almach**, the star at the left-hand end of the line. It's a beautiful double star. The main star is a yellow supergiant shining 650 times brighter than the Sun, and its companion – which is 5th magnitude – is bluish. The two stars are a lovely sight in small telescopes. Almach is actually a quadruple star: its companion is in fact triple.

But the glory of Andromeda is its great galaxy, beautifully placed on October nights. Lying above the line of stars, the **Andromeda Galaxy** is the most distant object visible to the unaided eye. It lies a mind-boggling 2.5 million light years away, yet it's so vast that it appears nearly four times as big as the Full Moon in the sky (although the sky will seldom be clear enough to allow you to see the faint outer spiral arms).

The Andromeda Galaxy is the biggest member of the Local Group – it is estimated to contain over 400 billion stars. It's a wonderful sight in binoculars or a small telescope, and the latter will reveal its two bright companion galaxies – M32 and NGC205.

WEST

OPHIUCHUS
AQUILA
CORONA BOREALIS
HERCULES
LYRA
THE MILKY WAY
CYGNUS
Vega
BOÖTES
DRACO
Deneb
CANES VENATICI
The Plough
CEPHEUS
Zenith
CASSIOPEIA
Almach
Algol
NORTH
URSA MINOR
Polaris
PERSEUS
URSA MAJOR
Capella
7 Oct
AURIGA
Castor
GEMINI
10 Oct
Radiant of Orionids
Ecliptic
Aldebaran
Pollux
Betelgeuse
ORION
NE
NW

EAST

the beginning of October, and 9 pm at the end of the month (after the end of BST). The planets move slightly relative to the stars during the month.

PLANETS ON VIEW

Jupiter is still brilliant (magnitude −2.5) in the south-west evening sky, in Capricornus. By the end of October, it's setting before midnight; but with the earlier sunsets at this time of year, the giant planet is still dominant for first five hours of darkness.

Capricornus is also hosting distant **Neptune**, with a sub-naked-eye magnitude of +7.9.

Uranus is technically just visible to the unaided eye, at magnitude +5.7. But it's much more easily found in binoculars or a telescope, right on the border of Aquarius and Pisces. Uranus sets at 5.50 am at the beginning of October, and 2.45 am at the end of the month.

Stay up until midnight, and you'll see **Mars** rising in the north-east. During October, the Red Planet scoots from Gemini into Cancer, gradually brightening from magnitude +0.8 to +0.4. In the first two weeks of October, the Red Planet forms a slightly brighter 'triplet' to the twin stars Castor (+1.6) and Pollux (+1.2). At the end of the month it crosses the Praesepe star cluster (see Special Events).

There's a fascinating planetary dance going on in the pre-dawn sky. The major player is **Venus**. The brilliant Morning Star (magnitude −3.9) rises at 4.40 am at the start of the month, and 5.10 am by month-end, when it's sinking into the dawn glow.

October gives us the best chance of the year to see **Mercury** in the morning sky: the innermost planet is at greatest western elongation on 6 October. At the start of the month, you'll find

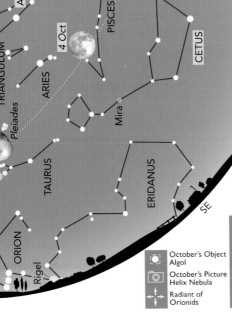

WEST

SERPENS

THE MILKY WAY

AQUILA

CYGNUS

SAGITTA

Altair

DELPHINUS

Deneb

Enif

AQUARIUS

Neptune Jupiter

25 Oct

CAPRICORNUS

PISCIS AUSTRINUS

Helix Nebula

1 Oct

CASSIOPEIA

Zenith

Andromeda Galaxy

PEGASUS

Square of Pegasus

ANDROMEDA

PERSEUS

Almach

Algol

TRIANGULUM

PISCES

Ecliptic

Uranus

4 Oct

Fomalhaut

SOUTH

7 Oct

Pleiades

ARIES

Mira

CETUS

Aldebaran

TAURUS

ERIDANUS

Betelgeuse

ORION

Rigel

SE

EAST

Jupiter

Uranus

Neptune

Moon

October's Object
Algol

October's Picture
Helix Nebula

Radiant of
Orionids

MOON		
Date	Time	Phase
4	7.10 am	Full Moon
11	9.56 am	Last Quarter
18	6.33 am	New Moon
26	0.42 am	First Quarter

Mercury to the lower left of Venus, rising around 5.30 am and shining at magnitude +0.4. Over the next two weeks, it brightens to magnitude −1.0.

At the beginning of October, slightly fainter **Saturn** (magnitude +1.1) lies to the lower left of Mercury. These three planets converge as the days pass. On the morning of 8 October, Saturn and Mercury lie only a third of a degree apart, 5 degrees to the lower left of Venus. Saturn continues to move upwards, and the ringed planet lies only half a degree from Venus on the mornings of 13 and 14 October (on the latter date telescopic observers can see Saturn hide its largest moon – see Special Events). Through a small telescope, you'll notice that Saturn's famous rings appear very narrow, as we are seeing them almost edge-on. The Earth actually passed through the ring-plane in September, when Saturn was too close to the Sun to be seen.

MOON

On 7 October, the Moon skims the Pleiades (Seven Sisters) star cluster. The Last Quarter Moon lies just over a degree from Mars on the morning of 12 October. In the morning of 14 October, the Moon lies near Regulus in Leo. The narrow crescent Moon forms a striking pair with Venus just before dawn on 16 October, with Saturn to the upper left and Mercury down near the horizon. On the evening of 21 October, the crescent Moon is very close to Antares. Jupiter is near the Moon on 26 and 27 October; on the latter date, the Moon passes just over a degree from Neptune.

SPECIAL EVENTS

On the morning of **14 October**, observers with reasonably powerful telescopes have an opportunity to see Saturn's biggest moon, Titan, passing behind the planet's north polar region. The occultation is under way when Saturn rises at 5.15 am, and finishes around 7.10 am when the planet is lost in the dawn brightness.

Debris from Halley's Comet smashes into Earth's atmosphere on **20/21 October**, causing the annual **Orionid** meteor shower.

At 2 am on **25 October**, we see the end of British Summer Time for this year. Clocks go backwards by an hour.

24 October–1 November is Moonwatch Week (Autumn), part of the International Year of Astronomy celebrations. Organized star parties will be homing in on the Moon and Jupiter.

On the nights of **30/31 October** and **31 October/1 November**, Mars moves right in front of the Praesepe

(Beehive) star cluster in Cancer – a lovely sight in binoculars or a small telescope.

OCTOBER'S OBJECT

The star **Algol**, in the constellation **Perseus**, represents the head of the dreadful Gorgon Medusa. In Arabic, its name means 'the Demon'. Watch Algol carefully and you'll see why. Every 2 days 21 hours, Algol dims in brightness for several hours, to become as faint as the star lying to its lower right (Gorgonea Tertia).

In 1783, John Goodricke of York, a young British amateur astronomer, discovered Algol's regular changes, and proposed that Algol is orbited by a large dark planet that periodically blocks off some of its light. We now know that Algol does indeed have a dim companion blocking its brilliant light, but it's a fainter star rather than a planet.

OCTOBER'S PICTURE

The glorious **Helix Nebula** in **Aquarius** is one of the sky's most stunning sights, but it's a chilling reminder of the mortality of the Sun. When our star's nuclear reactions cease – in, perhaps, 7 billion years' time – it will eject its atmosphere into space, probably incinerating the Earth. All that will be left will be a rapidly-cooling white dwarf star, at the centre of the tendrils of gas.

⊙ Viewing tip

Around 2.5 million light years away from us, the Andromeda Galaxy is often described as the furthest object easily visible to the unaided eye. But it's not that easy to see – especially if you are suffering some light pollution. The trick is to memorize the star patterns in Andromeda and look slightly to the side of where you expect the galaxy to be. This technique – called 'averted vision' – causes the image to fall on parts of the retina that are more light-sensitive than the central region, which is designed to see fine detail.

OCTOBER'S TOPIC
Mars Science Laboratory

If all goes according to plan, this month should see the Mars Science Laboratory on its way to the Red Planet. Due to land in autumn 2010, the MSL spaceprobe is NASA's most ambitious robotic mission to Mars since Viking in 1976. It will scour our neighbour's surface for a full Martian year – 687 Earth days – although, if the rovers Spirit and Opportunity are anything to go by, it should last a lot longer.

The six-wheeled, 1-tonne rover, the size of a people-carrier, will pave the way to tracking down life on the Red Planet. It's NASA's boldest Mars mission to date – in the words of a spokesperson: 'Our biggest, baddest, newest rover'.

MSL is three times heavier than any rover that's been sent to Mars before. It will also outperform its predecessors. Travelling at up to 90 metres per hour, it will be able to roll over obstacles as high as 75 centimetres.

It has an exquisite suite of scientific instruments. Its cameras – built by Malin Space Systems – will be second-to-none. MSL also boasts a water detector from Russia, and a sophisticated laser system to vaporize the Martian soil – and analyze it for atoms of life-providing carbon.

When we see the **Pleiades**, we know that winter is upon us. 'A swarm of fireflies tangled in a silver braid' was the evocative description of the glittering star cluster by Alfred, Lord Tennyson, in his 1842 poem 'Locksley Hall'. Throughout history, and all over the world, people have been intrigued by this lovely sight. Amazingly, from Greece to Australia, ancient myths independently describe the stars as a group of young girls being chased by an aggressive male – often **Aldebaran** or **Orion** – hence giving rise to the cluster's popular name, the 'Seven Sisters'. Polynesian navigators used the Pleiades to mark the start of their year. And farmers in the Andes rely on the visibility of the Pleiades as a guide to planting their potatoes: the brightness or faintness of the Seven Sisters depends on El Niño, which affects the forthcoming weather.

▼ The sky at 10 pm in mid-November, with Moon positions at three-day intervals either side of Full Moon. The star positions are also correct for 11 pm at

NOVEMBER'S CONSTELLATION

Up in the northern sky hangs a star-pattern making the unmistakable shape of a capital 'W'. To the ancients, this constellation represented Queen **Cassiopeia** of Ethiopia, who ruled with her husband, King **Cepheus**.

Cassiopeia misguidedly boasted that her daughter **Andromeda** was more beautiful than the sea nymphs. Poseidon, the sea god, was so incensed that he sent a ravaging monster (**Cetus**). It could only be appeased by the sacrifice of Andromeda – but she was rescued by the hero **Perseus**. Cepheus, Andromeda and Perseus are also immortalized by constellations lying near to Cassiopeia.

The Chinese saw Cassiopeia as three star groups, including a chariot and a mountain path. Unusually, the central star in Cassiopeia is known today by its Chinese name – **Tsih** (the Whip). This star is unstable in brightness. Some 70,000 times brighter than the Sun, it spins around at breakneck pace, flinging out streams of gas.

the beginning of November, and 9 pm at the end of the month. The planets move slightly relative to the stars during the month.

Cassiopeia has seen two more extreme variable stars – supernovae, where an entire star has blown apart. One was seen by Danish astronomer Tycho Brahe in 1572. The other exploded around 1660 as a surprisingly dim supernova, but its expanding gases form the most prominent radio source in the sky, Cassiopeia A.

PLANETS ON VIEW

Jupiter lords it over the evening sky, at magnitude −2.3 in Capricornus. The giant planet sets at 11.15 pm at the start of November, and 9.40 pm by the month's end. Use binoculars or a small telescope to spot its four biggest moons.

The most distant planet, **Neptune** (magnitude +7.9), also lies in Capricornus, setting about half an hour after Jupiter.

Where Aquarius abuts Pisces, you'll find **Uranus**, at magnitude +5.8. Its setting time advances from 2.45 am to 0.45 am during November.

Mars is making a dramatic entrance on to the evening-sky panorama. At the beginning of November, it appears in the north-east at 10 pm, moving to 9 pm by the end of the month. During November, the Red Planet brightens from magnitude +0.4 to 0.0, as it moves from Cancer (where it starts the month in Praesepe – see Special Events) towards Leo.

In the small hours, you'll find **Saturn** (magnitude +1.0) rising in the east – in Virgo – around 3.15 am at

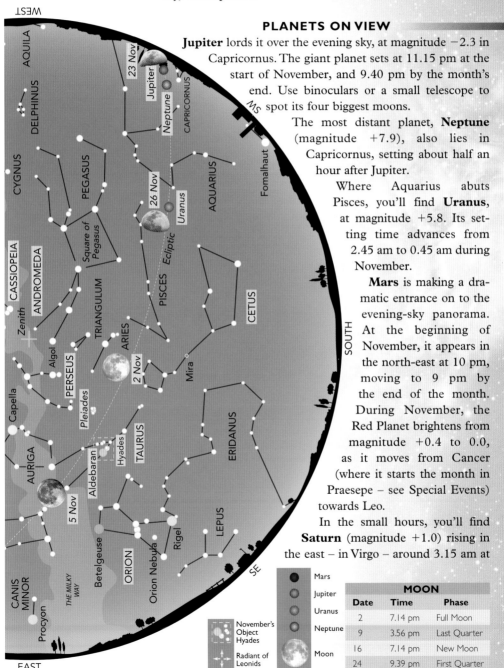

		MOON	
	Date	**Time**	**Phase**
	2	7.14 pm	Full Moon
	9	3.56 pm	Last Quarter
	16	7.14 pm	New Moon
	24	9.39 pm	First Quarter

the start of November, and 1.30 am at the end of the month. Its famous rings appear narrow, but they are gradually broadening as we move away from the 'edge-on' position.

Venus is now in the dawn glow, but still easily visible at magnitude −3.9. The Morning Star is rising at 5.15 am at the beginning of the month, and 6.45 am at the end of November. For the first few days of November, it lies near Spica.

Mercury is too close to the Sun to be seen in November.

MOON

In the early hours of 4 November, the Moon passes just under the Seven Sisters – the Pleiades star cluster. The Moon lies near Mars on the night of 8/9 November, while the crescent Moon passes Saturn on the morning of 13 November and Venus just before dawn on 15 November. On 23 November, the Moon lies near Jupiter.

SPECIAL EVENTS

On the nights of **1/2** and **2/3 November**, you'll find Mars in front of the Praesepe (Beehive) star cluster in Cancer – check it out with binoculars or a small telescope.

17 November sees the maximum of the **Leonid** meteor shower. A few years ago, this annual shower yielded literally storms of shooting stars, but the rate has gone down as the parent Comet Tempel-Tuttle, which sheds its dust to produce the meteors, has moved away from the vicinity of Earth.

◉ *Viewing tip*

Now that the nights are drawing in earlier, and becoming darker, it's a good time to pick out faint, fuzzy objects like the Andromeda Galaxy and the Orion Nebula. But don't even think about it near the time of Full Moon – its light will drown them out. The best time to observe 'deep-sky objects' is when the Moon is near to New, or after Full Moon. Check the Moon phases timetable in the book.

NOVEMBER'S TOPIC
Galaxies

With the Andromeda Galaxy riding high, and the stars of our own Galaxy all around us, it's time to take a look at the billions of star-cities that populate the Universe. Both the Milky Way and the Andromeda Galaxy are 'spirals' – they're rich in gas and dust, poised to make new generations of stars, and adorned with beautiful curving arms made of young, hot stars. Irregular galaxies have a similar mix of ingredients, but are too small to 'grow' arms. If you visit the Southern Hemisphere, you can see our two irregular companions, the Large and Small Magellanic Clouds, shining brightly in the sky. 'Ellipticals' make up the third category of galaxy. These range from the very small to the truly gargantuan, some with trillions of stars. But most of those stars are old and red; there's very little by way of building materials in these galaxies to make new stars. A few galaxies are violent, with brilliant jets of gas shooting out from the vicinity of a central black hole at speeds close to the velocity of light.

NOVEMBER'S OBJECT

The V-shaped **Hyades** star cluster, which forms the 'head' of **Taurus** (the Bull), doesn't hold a candle to the dazzling **Pleiades**. But it's the nearest star cluster to the Earth, and it forms the first rung of the ladder in establishing the cosmic distance scale. By measuring the speeds of the stars in the cluster, astronomers can establish their properties, and use these to find the distances to stars that are further away.

In legend, the Hyades feature in many myths – often as female figures (for example, the nymphs who cared for Bacchus as a baby). But the interpretations we like most are those of the Romans, who called the stars 'little pigs', and the Chinese vision of them as a 'rabbit net'.

Although **Aldebaran**, marking the bull's angry eye, looks as though it is part of the Hyades, this red giant just happens to lie in the same direction, and at less than half the distance.

The Hyades cluster lies 151 light years away (that's the latest Hipparcos satellite distance), and contains about 200 stars. The stars are all around 790 million years old – quite young on the stellar scale – and they may have a celestial twin. It turns out that the **Praesepe** (Beehive) star cluster, in Cancer, is the same age, and its stars are moving in the same direction. It may well be that the two clusters share a common birth.

NOVEMBER'S PICTURE

Our cratered satellite, viewed in close-up. You can see the Moon's pockmarked surface and 'seas' with the unaided eye, but binoculars bring it closer. Using a small telescope makes it feel as if you are flying over our neighbour-world. In this image, the large dark circular 'sea' is Mare Crisium – the result of an asteroid impact that took place 3.8 billion years ago.

It's the month of the shortest day – and the longest night. On 21 December, we hit the Winter Solstice – the nadir of the year, which has long been commemorated in tablets of stone aligned to welcome the returning Sun. But the darkness brings with it a welcome fireworks display of meteors on 13 December, as the **Geminids** streak into our atmosphere. The shooting stars are debris shed from an asteroid called Phaethon, and therefore quite substantial – and hence bright. This is a good year for observing them, as moonlight won't interfere.

DECEMBER'S CONSTELLATION

Taurus is very much a second cousin to brilliant **Orion**, but is a fascinating constellation, nonetheless. It is dominated by **Aldebaran**, the baleful blood-red eye of the celestial bull. Around 68 light years away, and shining with a magnitude of +0.85, Aldebaran is a red giant star, but not one as extreme as neighbouring **Betelgeuse**. Aldebaran is around three times heavier than the Sun. The 'head' of the bull is formed by the **Hyades** star cluster. The other famous star cluster in Taurus is the far more glamorous **Pleiades**, whose stars – although further away than the Hyades – are younger and brighter.

Taurus has two 'horns' – the star **El Nath** (Arabic for 'the butting one') to the north, and **zeta Tauri** (which has an unpronounceable Babylonian name meaning 'star in the bull towards the south'). Above this star is a stellar wreck – literally. In 1054, Chinese astronomers witnessed a brilliant 'new star' appear in this spot, which was visible in daytime for weeks. What the Chinese actually saw was an exploding star – a supernova – in its death throes. And today, we see its still-expanding remains as the **Crab Nebula**. It's visible through a medium-sized telescope.

▼ *The sky at 10 pm in mid-December, with Moon positions at three-day intervals either side of Full Moon. The star positions are also correct for 11 pm at the beginning of December, and 9 pm at the end of the month. The planets move slightly relative to the stars during the month.*

PLANETS ON VIEW

In the week before Christmas, you may spot elusive **Mercury** (magnitude 0.0) low in the south-west after sunset. It is at greatest eastern elongation on 18 December.

The brightest of the outer planets, **Jupiter**, and the faintest – **Neptune** – still reside in Capricornus and set around 9 pm (too early to show on the chart). You can't miss Jupiter, at magnitude −2.2. Neptune, at magnitude +7.9, requires a telescope. The planets pass on 21 December (see Special Events).

Uranus (magnitude +5.9), on the borders of Aquarius and Pisces, sets around 11.45 pm.

Mars is now steaming full-speed on to the celestial stage. During December, it brightens from magnitude 0.0 to −0.8, to outshine all the stars apart from Sirius. The Red Planet lies between Leo and Cancer, and rises around 8 pm.

Rising in the south-east about 0.45 am, you'll find ringworld **Saturn** (magnitude +1.0) lying in the constellation Virgo.

Venus is lost in the predawn twilight glow this month.

MOON

The Moon lies near Mars on 6 December, and Regulus on 7 December. It passes Saturn on the morning of 10 December. Early on 11 and 12 December, the star near the Moon is Spica. Just after sunset on 18 December, the narrow crescent Moon lies to the upper left of Mercury. On 21 December, the Moon is near Jupiter and Neptune.

Chart labels: WEST, AQUARIUS, PEGASUS, Uranus, Ecliptic, 24 Dec, Square of Pegasus, ANDROMEDA, PISCES, CETUS, TRIANGULUM, 27 Dec, ARIES, Mira, Algol, Zenith, PERSEUS, Pleiades, Hyades, TAURUS, ERIDANUS, Capella, AURIGA, AE Aurigae, El Nath, zeta Tauri, Aldebaran, Betelgeuse, Rigel, LEPUS, Radiant of Geminids, Castor, Pollux, Crab Nebula, 2 Dec, Orion Nebula, ORION, CANIS MAJOR, COLUMBA, GEMINI, Procyon, CANIS MINOR, THE MILKY WAY, Sirius, Adhara, 5 Dec, CANCER, HYDRA, EAST, SE, SOUTH, MS

Legend:
December's Object Orion Nebula
December's Picture AE Aurigae
Radiant of Geminids
Mars, Uranus, Moon

MOON		
Date	Time	Phase
2	7.30 am	Full Moon
9	0.13 am	Last Quarter
16	12.02 pm	New Moon
24	5.36 pm	First Quarter
31	7.13 pm	Full Moon

Just after midnight on 28/29 December, the Moon grazes the edge of the Pleiades.

SPECIAL EVENTS

The maximum of the **Geminid** meteor shower falls on **13/14 December**. These meteors are debris shed from an asteroid called Phaethon – they're quite substantial, and therefore bright. This is a good year to observe them, as the Moon will not interfere.

An excellent chance to identify Neptune comes on the evenings of **20** and **21 December**, when brilliant Jupiter passes nearby. With a telescope, locate Jupiter and then look upwards, at right angles to the line of Jupiter's moons, by half a degree to find Neptune. This is the final instalment of the triple conjunctions of Jupiter and Neptune this year (previous conjunctions were in May and July).

The Winter Solstice occurs at 5.47 pm on **21 December**. As a result of the tilt of Earth's axis, the Sun reaches its lowest point in the heavens as seen from the northern hemisphere: we get the shortest days, and the longest nights.

There's a partial eclipse of the Moon on **31 December**,

▲ *AE Aurigae and the surrounding Flaming Star Nebula: this image was made by Michael Stecker from California using an Astro-Physics 130 mm f/6 refractor. He combined two 50-minute exposures made on Fujicolor 400 film.*

though it will be easy to overlook as only 8% of the Moon's surface is hidden in the Earth's shadow. The eclipse begins at 6.52 pm and ends at 7.54 pm.

DECEMBER'S OBJECT

Look at Orion's Belt, and – on a clear night – you'll detect a small fuzzy patch below the line of stars. Through binoculars, or a small telescope, the patch looks like a small cloud in space. It is a cloud – but at 30 light years across, it's hardly small. Only the distance of the **Orion Nebula** – 1300 light years – diminishes it. Yet it is the nearest region of massive star formation to Earth, containing at least 150 fledgling stars (protostars), which have condensed out of the gas.

This 'star factory' is lit by fierce radiation from a small cluster of newly-born stars called 'the Trapezium', which are beautiful to look at through a small telescope. The Orion Nebula is just part of a huge gas complex in the Orion region which may have enough material to make 500,000 stars in the future.

DECEMBER'S PICTURE

The constellation of **Auriga** (the Charioteer) soars overhead this month. One of its highlights is **AE Aurigae**: a 6th-magnitude star that illuminates a patch of nebulosity, which appears in photographs to be immersed in flame. The star itself is a runaway from the Orion Nebula region – released from its orbit around another star when its companion exploded as a supernova.

DECEMBER'S TOPIC
Origin of the Universe

Christmas is on its way, with all its associations with birth and beginnings. But how did our Universe begin? Luckily, we have some pretty firm evidence to answer that question.

Firstly, the Universe is expanding – on the largest scales, galaxies are moving apart from each other. If you 'rewind the tape', you'll find that the expansion dates back to a time 13.7 billion years ago – a measurement that has only been tied down in recent years. Secondly, the Universe is not entirely cold – it is bathed in a radiation field of 2.7 degrees above Absolute Zero.

All of these clues point to the origin of the Universe in a blisteringly-hot 'Big Bang', which caused space to expand. The 'microwave background' of 2.7 degrees is the remnant of this birth in fire, cooled down by the relentless expansion to a mere shadow of its former self. Current observations show that the Universe is not just expanding, but *accelerating* – which means that it is destined to die by simply fading away.

There's always something to see in our Solar System, from planets to meteors or the Moon. These objects are very close to us – in astronomical terms – so their positions, shapes and sizes appear to change constantly. It is important to know when, where and how to look if you are to enjoy exploring Earth's neighbourhood. Here we give the best dates in 2009 for observing the planets and meteors (weather permitting!), and explain some of the concepts that will help you to get the most out of your observing.

THE INFERIOR PLANETS

A planet with an orbit that lies closer to the Sun than the orbit of Earth is known as *inferior*. Mercury and Venus are the inferior planets. They show a full range of phases (like the Moon) from the thinnest crescents to full, depending on their position in relation to the Earth and the Sun. The diagram below shows the various positions of the inferior planets. They are invisible when at *conjunction* and best viewed when at their eastern or western *elongations*.

Magnitudes

Astronomers measure the brightness of stars, planets and other celestial objects using a scale of *magnitudes*. Somewhat confusingly, fainter objects have higher magnitudes, while brighter objects have lower magnitudes; the most brilliant stars have negative magnitudes! Naked-eye stars range from magnitude −1.5 for the brightest star, Sirius, to +6.5 for the faintest stars you can see on a really dark night. As a guide, here are the magnitudes of selected objects:

Sun	−26.7
Full Moon	−12.5
Venus (at its brightest)	−4.6
Sirius	−1.5
Betelgeuse	+0.4
Polaris (Pole Star)	+2.0
Faintest star visible to the naked eye	+6.5
Faintest star visible to the Hubble Space Telescope	+31

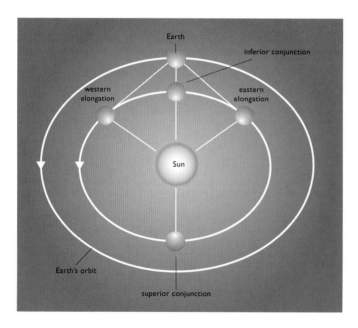

◀ At eastern or western elongation, an inferior planet is at its maximum angular distance from the Sun. Conjunction occurs at two stages in the planet's orbit. Under certain circumstances, an inferior planet can transit across the Sun's disc at inferior conjunction.

Mercury

In the first half of January, Mercury is visible in the dusk after sunset; it reaches its greatest eastern elongation on 4 January. From mid to end April is the best time to view the planet, low on the horizon between west and north-west in the evening twilight. In early October, Mercury has its best morning appearance, visible low in the east before sunrise. In mid December, the planet lies low in the south-west after sunset.

◉ Maximum elongations of Mercury in 2009	
Date	Separation
4 January	19.3° east
13 February	26.1° west
26 April	20.4° east
13 June	23.5° west
24 August	27.4° east
6 October	17.9° west
18 December	20.3° east

Maximum elongation of Venus in 2009	
Date	Separation
14 January	47.1° east
5 June	45.8° west

Venus

Venus reaches greatest eastern elongation on 14 January and greatest western elongation on 5 June. From January to March it is brilliant in the west as an Evening Star, disappearing from view at the end of March. It re-emerges as a Morning Star at the start of April, and reaches its best through August and September. It is lost from view in December.

THE SUPERIOR PLANETS

The superior planets are those with orbits that lie beyond that of the Earth. They are Mars, Jupiter, Saturn, Uranus and Neptune. The best time to observe a superior planet is when the Earth lies between it and the Sun. At this point in the planet's orbit, it is said to be at *opposition*.

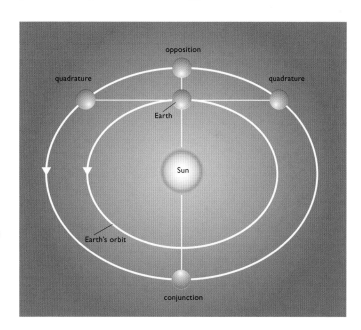

▶ Superior planets are invisible at conjunction. At quadrature the planet is at right angles to the Sun as viewed from Earth. Opposition is the best time to observe a superior planet.

Mars

Mars is lost from view from January to the end of May, when it rises higher in the sky and is more easily seen in the dawn twilight. By the end of June, it is rising at around 2.00 am but is still quite dim; Venus passes close by on the mornings of 21 and 22 June. By December, though, Mars is brighter than all the stars apart from Sirius and rises at around 8 pm.

Jupiter

Jupiter is best placed for observing from late summer to the end of the year. During August it is the brightest object in Capricornus, shining low in the south around midnight and visible all night long. It reaches opposition on 14 August.

Saturn

Saturn is in Leo until September, when it moves into Virgo. It is at opposition on 8 March, and is at its best for observing from January to June.

Uranus

Uranus is best viewed from July onwards, when it lies on the border of Aquarius and Pisces. Visibility improves into the months of autumn, and it reaches opposition on 17 September.

Neptune

Neptune spends 2009 in Capricornus and is best viewed from June onwards. Conjunctions with Jupiter occur on 28 May, 10 July and 21 December; it reaches opposition on 17 August.

SOLAR AND LUNAR ECLIPSES

Solar Eclipses

There are two solar eclipses in 2009, on 26 January and 22 July. The former is annular, and can be seen from the Indian Ocean and Indonesia, and will be partial over southern Africa and western Australia. The latter is total, and is visible from India, Burma (Myanmar) and China, ending in the Pacific. It will be visible as a partial eclipse over south-east and eastern Asia, and most of Indonesia.

Lunar Eclipses

There will be a minor partial lunar eclipse on 31 December 2009 – New Year's Eve. The greatest part of the eclipse will occur at 7.23 pm. However, only 8% of the Moon's surface will be hidden in the Earth's shadow.

Astronomical distances

For objects in the Solar System, such as the planets, we can give their distances from the Earth in kilometres. But the distances are just too huge once we reach out to the stars. Even the nearest star (Proxima Centauri) lies 25 million million kilometres away.

So astronomers use a larger unit – the *light year*. This is the distance that light travels in one year, and it equals 9.46 million million kilometres. Here are the distances to some familiar astronomical objects, in light years:

Proxima Centauri	4.2
Betelgeuse	427
Centre of the Milky Way	26,000
Andromeda Galaxy	2.5 million
Most distant galaxies seen by the Hubble Space Telescope	13 billion

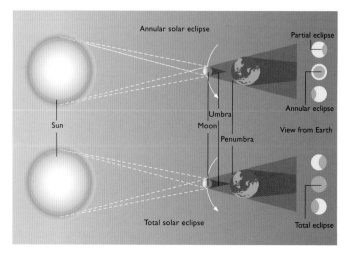

◄ Where the dark central part (the umbra) of the Moon's shadow reaches the Earth, a total eclipse is seen. People located within the penumbra see a partial eclipse. If the umbral shadow does not reach Earth, an annular eclipse is seen. This type of eclipse occurs when the Moon is at a distant point in its orbit and is not quite large enough to cover the whole of the Sun's disc.

Dates of maximum for selected meteor showers	
Meteor shower	Date of maximum
Quadrantids	3/4 January
Lyrids	21/22 April
Eta Aquarids	4/5 May
Perseids	12/13 August
Orionids	20/21 October
Leonids	17/18 November
Geminids	13/14 December

▶ *Meteors from a common source, occurring during a shower, enter the atmosphere along parallel trajectories. As a result of perspective, however, they appear to diverge from a single point in the sky – the radiant.*

METEOR SHOWERS

Shooting stars – or *meteors* – are tiny particles of interplanetary dust, known as *meteoroids*, burning up in the Earth's atmosphere. At certain times of year, the Earth passes through a stream of these meteoroids (usually debris left behind by a comet) and a *meteor shower* is seen. The point in the sky from which the meteors appear to emanate is known as the *radiant*. Most showers are known by the constellation in which the radiant is situated.

observer's field of view

When watching meteors for a coordinated meteor programme, observers generally note the time, seeing conditions, cloud cover, their own location, the time and brightness of each meteor, and whether it was from the main meteor stream. It is also worth noting details of persistent afterglows (trains) and fireballs, and making counts of how many meteors appear in a given period.

Angular separations

Astronomers measure the distance between objects, as we see them in the sky, by the angle between the objects in degrees (symbol °). From the horizon to the point above your head is 90 degrees. All around the horizon is 360 degrees.
You can use your hand, held at arm's length, as a rough guide to angular distances, as follows:
Width of index finger   1°
Width of clenched hand 10°
Thumb to little finger
  on outspread hand   20°
For smaller distances, astronomers divide the degree into 60 arcminutes (symbol '), and the arcminute into 60 arcseconds (symbol ").

COMETS

Comets are small bodies in orbit about the Sun. Consisting of frozen gases and dust, they are often known as 'dirty snowballs'. When their orbits bring them close to the Sun, the ices evaporate and dramatic tails of gas and dust can sometimes be seen.

A number of comets move round the Sun in fairly small, elliptical orbits in periods of a few years; others have much longer periods. Most really brilliant comets have orbital periods of several thousands or even millions of years. The exception is Comet Halley, a bright comet with a period of about 76 years. It was last seen with the naked eye in 1986.

Binoculars and wide-field telescopes provide the best views of comet tails. Larger telescopes with a high magnification are necessary to observe fine detail in the gaseous head (*coma*). Most comets are discovered with professional instruments, but a few are still found by experienced amateur astronomers.

None of the known comets is predicted to reach naked-eye brightness in 2009, but there's always a chance of a bright new comet putting in a surprise appearance.

Deep-sky objects are 'fuzzy patches' that lie outside the Solar System. They include star clusters, nebulae and galaxies. To observe the majority of deep-sky objects you will need binoculars or a telescope, but there are also some beautiful naked-eye objects, notably the Pleiades and the Orion Nebula.

The faintest object that an instrument can see is its *limiting magnitude*. The table gives a rough guide, for good seeing conditions, for a variety of small- to medium-sized telescopes.

We have provided a selection of recommended deep-sky targets, together with their magnitudes. Some are described in more detail in our 'Object of the Month' features. Look on the appropriate month's map to find which constellations are on view, and then choose your objects using the list below. We have provided celestial coordinates for readers with detailed star maps. The suggested times of year for viewing are when the constellation is highest in the sky in the late evening.

| Limiting magnitude for small to medium telescopes ||
Aperture (mm)	Limiting magnitude
50	+11.2
60	+11.6
70	+11.9
80	+12.2
100	+12.7
125	+13.2
150	+13.6

RECOMMENDED DEEP-SKY OBJECTS

Andromeda – autumn and early winter

M31 (NGC 224) Andromeda Galaxy	3rd-magnitude spiral galaxy RA 00h 42.7m Dec +41° 16'
M32 (NGC 221)	8th-magnitude elliptical galaxy, a companion to M31 RA 00h 42.7m Dec +40° 52'
M110 (NGC 205)	8th-magnitude elliptical galaxy RA 00h 40.4m Dec +41° 41'
NGC 7662 Blue Snowball	8th-magnitude planetary nebula RA 23h 25.9m Dec +42° 33'

Aquarius – late autumn and early winter

M2 (NGC 7089)	6th-magnitude globular cluster RA 21h 33.5m Dec –00° 49'
M72 (NGC 6981)	9th-magnitude globular cluster RA 20h 53.5m Dec –12° 32'
NGC 7293 Helix Nebula	7th-magnitude planetary nebula RA 22h 29.6m Dec –20° 48'
NGC 7009 Saturn Nebula	8th-magnitude planetary nebula RA 21h 04.2m Dec –11° 22'

Aries – early winter

NGC 772	10th-magnitude spiral galaxy RA 01h 59.3m Dec +19° 01'

Auriga – winter

M36 (NGC 1960)	6th-magnitude open cluster RA 05h 36.1m Dec +34° 08'
M37 (NGC 2099)	6th-magnitude open cluster RA 05h 52.4m Dec +32° 33'
M38 (NGC 1912)	6th-magnitude open cluster RA 05h 28.7m Dec +35° 50'

Cancer – late winter to early spring

M44 (NGC 2632) Praesepe or Beehive	3rd-magnitude open cluster RA 08h 40.1m Dec +19° 59'
M67 (NGC 2682)	7th-magnitude open cluster RA 08h 50.4m Dec +11° 49'

Canes Venatici – visible all year

M3 (NGC 5272)	6th-magnitude globular cluster RA 13h 42.2m Dec +28° 23'
M51 (NGC 5194/5) Whirlpool Galaxy	8th-magnitude spiral galaxy RA 13h 29.9m Dec +47° 12'
M63 (NGC 5055)	9th-magnitude spiral galaxy RA 13h 15.8m Dec +42° 02'
M94 (NGC 4736)	8th-magnitude spiral galaxy RA 12h 50.9m Dec +41° 07'
M106 (NGC4258)	8th-magnitude spiral galaxy RA 12h 19.0m Dec +47° 18'

Canis Major – late winter

M41 (NGC 2287)	4th-magnitude open cluster RA 06h 47.0m Dec –20° 44'

Capricornus – late summer and early autumn

M30 (NGC 7099)	7th-magnitude globular cluster RA 21h 40.4m Dec –23° 11'

Cassiopeia – visible all year

M52 (NGC 7654)	6th-magnitude open cluster RA 23h 24.2m Dec +61° 35'
M103 (NGC 581)	7th-magnitude open cluster RA 01h 33.2m Dec +60° 42'
NGC 225	7th-magnitude open cluster RA 00h 43.4m Dec +61 47'
NGC 457	6th-magnitude open cluster RA 01h 19.1m Dec +58° 20'
NGC 663	Good binocular open cluster RA 01h 46.0m Dec +61° 15'

Cepheus – visible all year

Delta Cephei	Variable star, varying between +3.5 and +4.4 with a period of 5.37 days. It has a magnitude +6.3 companion and they make an attractive pair for small telescopes or binoculars.

Cetus – late autumn

Mira (omicron Ceti)	Irregular variable star with a period of roughly 330 days and a range between +2.0 and +10.1.
M77 (NGC 1068)	9th-magnitude spiral galaxy RA 02h 42.7m Dec –00° 01'

Coma Berenices – spring

M53 (NGC 5024)	8th-magnitude globular cluster RA 13h 12.9m Dec +18° 10'
M64 (NGC 4286) Black Eye Galaxy	8th-magnitude spiral galaxy with a prominent dust lane that is visible in larger telescopes. RA 12h 56.7m Dec +21° 41'
M85 (NGC 4382)	9th-magnitude elliptical galaxy RA 12h 25.4m Dec +18° 11'
M88 (NGC 4501)	10th-magnitude spiral galaxy RA 12h 32.0m Dec.+14° 25'
M91 (NGC 4548)	10th-magnitude spiral galaxy RA 12h 35.4m Dec +14° 30'
M98 (NGC 4192)	10th-magnitude spiral galaxy RA 12h 13.8m Dec +14° 54'
M99 (NGC 4254)	10th-magnitude spiral galaxy RA 12h 18.8m Dec +14° 25'
M100 (NGC 4321)	9th-magnitude spiral galaxy RA 12h 22.9m Dec +15° 49'
NGC 4565	10th-magnitude spiral galaxy RA 12h 36.3m Dec +25° 59'

Cygnus – late summer and autumn

Cygnus Rift	Dark cloud just south of Deneb that appears to split the Milky Way in two.
NGC 7000 North America Nebula	A bright nebula against the background of the Milky Way, visible with binoculars under dark skies. RA 20h 58.8m Dec +44° 20'
NGC 6992 Veil Nebula (part)	Supernova remnant, visible with binoculars under dark skies. RA 20h 56.8m Dec +31 28'
M29 (NGC 6913)	7th-magnitude open cluster RA 20h 23.9m Dec +36° 32'
M39 (NGC 7092)	Large 5th-magnitude open cluster RA 21h 32.2m Dec +48° 26'
NGC 6826 Blinking Planetary	9th-magnitude planetary nebula RA 19 44.8m Dec +50° 31'

Delphinus – late summer

NGC 6934	9th-magnitude globular cluster RA 20h 34.2m Dec +07° 24'

Draco – midsummer

NGC 6543	9th-magnitude planetary nebula RA 17h 58.6m Dec +66° 38'

Gemini – winter

M35 (NGC 2168)	5th-magnitude open cluster RA 06h 08.9m Dec +24° 20'
NGC 2392 Eskimo Nebula	8–10th-magnitude planetary nebula RA 07h 29.2m Dec +20° 55'

Hercules – early summer

M13 (NGC 6205)	6th-magnitude globular cluster RA 16h 41.7m Dec +36° 28'
M92 (NGC 6341)	6th-magnitude globular cluster RA 17h 17.1m Dec +43° 08'
NGC 6210	9th-magnitude planetary nebula RA 16h 44.5m Dec +23 49'

Hydra – early spring

M48 (NGC 2548)	6th-magnitude open cluster RA 08h 13.8m Dec –05° 48'
M68 (NGC 4590)	8th-magnitude globular cluster RA 12h 39.5m Dec –26° 45'

M83 (NGC 5236)

M83 (NGC 5236)	8th-magnitude spiral galaxy RA 13h 37.0m Dec –29° 52'
NGC 3242 Ghost of Jupiter	9th-magnitude planetary nebula RA 10h 24.8m Dec –18°38'

Leo – spring

M65 (NGC 3623)	9th-magnitude spiral galaxy RA 11h 18.9m Dec +13° 05'
M66 (NGC 3627)	9th-magnitude spiral galaxy RA 11h 20.2m Dec +12° 59'
M95 (NGC 3351)	10th-magnitude spiral galaxy RA 10h 44.0m Dec +11° 42'
M96 (NGC 3368)	9th-magnitude spiral galaxy RA 10h 46.8m Dec +11° 49'
M105 (NGC 3379)	9th-magnitude elliptical galaxy RA 10h 47.8m Dec +12° 35'

Lepus – winter

M79 (NGC 1904)	8th-magnitude globular cluster RA 05h 24.5m Dec –24° 33'

Lyra – spring

M56 (NGC 6779)	8th-magnitude globular cluster RA 19h 16.6m Dec +30° 11'
M57 (NGC 6720) Ring Nebula	9th-magnitude planetary nebula RA 18h 53.6m Dec +33° 02'

Monoceros – winter

M50 (NGC 2323)	6th-magnitude open cluster RA 07h 03.2m Dec –08° 20'
NGC 2244	Open cluster surrounded by the faint Rosette Nebula, NGC 2237. Visible in binoculars. RA 06h 32.4m Dec +04° 52'

Ophiuchus – summer

M9 (NGC 6333)	8th-magnitude globular cluster RA 17h 19.2m Dec –18° 31'
M10 (NGC 6254)	7th-magnitude globular cluster RA 16h 57.1m Dec –04° 06'
M12 (NCG 6218)	7th-magnitude globular cluster RA 16h 47.2m Dec –01° 57'
M14 (NGC 6402)	8th-magnitude globular cluster RA 17h 37.6m Dec –03° 15'
M19 (NGC 6273)	7th-magnitude globular cluster RA 17h 02.6m Dec –26° 16'
M62 (NGC 6266)	7th-magnitude globular cluster RA 17h 01.2m Dec –30° 07'
M107 (NGC 6171)	8th-magnitude globular cluster RA 16h 32.5m Dec –13° 03'

Orion – winter

M42 (NGC 1976) Orion Nebula	4th-magnitude nebula RA 05h 35.4m Dec –05° 27'
M43 (NGC 1982)	5th-magnitude nebula RA 05h 35.6m Dec –05° 16'
M78 (NGC 2068)	8th-magnitude nebula RA 05h 46.7m Dec +00° 03'

Pegasus – autumn

M15 (NGC 7078)	6th-magnitude globular cluster RA 21h 30.0m Dec +12° 10'

Perseus – autumn to winter

M34 (NGC 1039)	5th-magnitude open cluster RA 02h 42.0m Dec +42° 47'
M76 (NGC 650/1) Little Dumbbell	11th-magnitude planetary nebula RA 01h 42.4m Dec +51° 34'

NGC 869/884 Double Cluster	Pair of open star clusters *RA 02h 19.0m Dec +57° 09'* *RA 02h 22.4m Dec +57° 07'*

Pisces – autumn

M74 (NGC 628)	9th-magnitude spiral galaxy *RA 01h 36.7m Dec +15° 47'*

Puppis – late winter

M46 (NGC 2437)	6th-magnitude open cluster *RA 07h 41.8m Dec –14° 49'*
M47 (NGC 2422)	4th-magnitude open cluster *RA 07h 36.6m Dec –14° 30'*
M93 (NGC 2447)	6th-magnitude open cluster *RA 07h 44.6m Dec –23° 52'*

Sagitta – late summer

M71 (NGC 6838)	8th-magnitude globular cluster *RA 19h 53.8m Dec +18° 47'*

Sagittarius – summer

M8 (NGC 6523) Lagoon Nebula	6th-magnitude nebula *RA 18h 03.8m Dec –24° 23'*
M17 (NGC 6618) Omega Nebula	6th-magnitude nebula *RA 18h 20.8m Dec –16° 11'*
M18 (NGC 6613)	7th-magnitude open cluster *RA 18h 19.9m Dec –17 08'*
M20 (NGC 6514) Trifid Nebula	9th-magnitude nebula *RA 18h 02.3m Dec –23° 02'*
M21 (NGC 6531)	6th-magnitude open cluster *RA 18h 04.6m Dec –22° 30'*
M22 (NGC 6656)	5th-magnitude globular cluster *RA 18h 36.4m Dec –23° 54'*
M23 (NGC 6494)	5th-magnitude open cluster *RA 17h 56.8m Dec –19° 01'*
M24 (NGC 6603)	5th-magnitude open cluster *RA 18h 16.9m Dec –18° 29'*
M25 (IC 4725)	5th-magnitude open cluster *RA 18h 31.6m Dec –19° 15'*
M28 (NGC 6626)	7th-magnitude globular cluster *RA 18h 24.5m Dec –24° 52'*
M54 (NGC 6715)	8th-magnitude globular cluster *RA 18h 55.1m Dec –30° 29'*
M55 (NGC 6809)	7th-magnitude globular cluster *RA 19h 40.0m Dec –30° 58'*
M69 (NGC 6637)	8th-magnitude globular cluster *RA 18h 31.4m Dec –32° 21'*
M70 (NGC 6681)	8th-magnitude globular cluster *RA 18h 43.2m Dec –32° 18'*
M75 (NGC 6864)	9th-magnitude globular cluster *RA 20h 06.1m Dec –21° 55'*

Scorpius (northern part) – midsummer

M4 (NGC 6121)	6th-magnitude globular cluster *RA 16h 23.6m Dec –26° 32'*
M7 (NGC 6475)	3rd-magnitude open cluster *RA 17h 53.9m Dec –34° 49'*
M80 (NGC 6093)	7th-magnitude globular cluster *RA 16h 17.0m Dec –22° 59'*

Scutum – mid to late summer

M11 (NGC 6705) Wild Duck Cluster	6th-magnitude open cluster *RA 18h 51.1m Dec –06° 16'*

M26 (NGC 6694)	8th-magnitude open cluster *RA 18h 45.2m Dec –09° 24'*

Serpens – summer

M5 (NGC 5904)	6th-magnitude globular cluster *RA 15h 18.6m Dec +02° 05'*
M16 (NGC 6611)	6th-magnitude open cluster, surrounded by the Eagle Nebula. *RA 18h 18.8m Dec –13° 47'*

Taurus – winter

M1 (NGC 1952) Crab Nebula	8th-magnitude supernova remnant *RA 05h 34.5m Dec +22° 00'*
M45 Pleiades	1st-magnitude open cluster, an excellent binocular object. *RA 03h 47.0m Dec +24° 07'*

Triangulum – autumn

M33 (NGC 598)	6th-magnitude spiral galaxy *RA 01h 33.9m Dec +30° 39'*

Ursa Major – all year

M81 (NGC 3031)	7th-magnitude spiral galaxy *RA 09h 55.6m Dec +69° 04'*
M82 (NGC 3034)	8th-magnitude starburst galaxy *RA 09h 55.8m Dec +69° 41'*
M97 (NGC 3587) Owl Nebula	12th-magnitude planetary nebula *RA 11h 14.8m Dec +55° 01'*
M101 (NGC 5457)	8th-magnitude spiral galaxy *RA 14h 03.2m Dec +54° 21'*
M108 (NGC 3556)	10th-magnitude spiral galaxy *RA 11h 11.5m Dec +55° 40'*
M109 (NGC 3992)	10th-magnitude spiral galaxy *RA 11h 57.6m Dec +53° 23'*

Virgo – spring

M49 (NGC 4472)	8th-magnitude elliptical galaxy *RA 12h 29.8m Dec +08° 00'*
M58 (NGC 4579)	10th-magnitude spiral galaxy *RA 12h 37.7m Dec +11° 49'*
M59 (NGC 4621)	10th-magnitude elliptical galaxy *RA 12h 42.0m Dec +11° 39'*
M60 (NGC 4649)	9th-magnitude elliptical galaxy *RA 12h 43.7m Dec +11° 33'*
M61 (NGC 4303)	10th-magnitude spiral galaxy *RA 12h 21.9m Dec +04° 28'*
M84 (NGC 4374)	9th-magnitude elliptical galaxy *RA 12h 25.1m Dec +12° 53'*
M86 (NGC 4406)	9th-magnitude elliptical galaxy *RA 12h 26.2m Dec +12° 57'*
M87 (NGC 4486)	9th-magnitude elliptical galaxy *RA 12h 30.8m Dec +12° 24'*
M89 (NGC 4552)	10th-magnitude elliptical galaxy *RA 12h 35.7m Dec +12° 33'*
M90 (NGC 4569)	9th-magnitude spiral galaxy *RA 12h 36.8m Dec +13° 10'*
M104 (NGC 4594) Sombrero Galaxy	Almost edge-on 8th-magnitude spiral galaxy. *RA 12h 40.0m Dec –11° 37'*

Vulpecula – late summer and autumn

M27 (NGC 6853) Dumbbell Nebula	8th-magnitude planetary nebula *RA 19h 59.6m Dec +22° 43'*

A t first sight, a GO TO telescope seems to be the ideal solution for anyone new to astronomy. These clever computer-controlled telescopes will find virtually any object in the sky for you at the touch of a button, then track it automatically as the sky turns. And these days they are not expensive, so they are definitely worth considering as a first telescope. But of course there are drawbacks, and you could end up with something that doesn't really do what you wanted, or is more complicated than you had hoped. This article looks at the GO TO systems from three major manufacturers – Celestron, Meade and Sky-Watcher. Each has a slightly different approach, and it's quite important to realize where the differences lie when you are considering one.

▲ *Three GO TO telescopes (L–R): Celestron CPC800 (200 mm) on altazimuth fork mount, £1,650; Meade LX90 (200 mm) on fork mount with equatorial wedge £1,750; Sky-Watcher Evostar 80ED2 Pro (80 mm) on German EQ5 mount, £820.*

The principle behind the way a GO TO telescope finds objects is quite simple and is similar to the way we find our way around any place we find ourselves in. If you've ever come out of a subway or underground station and looked around you to establish your bearings, you have done the same sort of thing. You find a feature you recognize, then another one, and once you have compared those with your mental map of the area, you should know where to find your actual destination. Because the sky is always moving, in the case of a telescope it needs to know where it is and the date and time, its orientation, and then the positions of some objects that it already has in its database. Once it knows these things, it should know where all the other objects are in the sky. The software also includes the means of calculating the positions of moving objects such as the Moon and planets for the time in question, so it can track down planets such as Uranus and Neptune.

So, although the telescopes are very clever once they are properly set up, they do have to know where they are and which way they are pointing first. This is where you, the user, has to get involved. Even though GPS units in some of them may help in setting some information, they all need to be pointed at particular stars in order to function accurately. The exact procedures vary from system to system, and they all place different demands on the user.

◄ *This Meade LX90 Schmidt-Cassegrain telescope with Autostar GO TO has been converted into an equatorial mount by means of the wedge between the base and the tripod, making it suitable for basic astrophotography. Recent models include GPS and PEC as standard.*

Three systems

One of the best-known systems is Meade's Autostar, used on their portable ETX telescopes and also on the larger LX90 series, as shown here. The Autostar system requires that the telescope starts by being level and pointing north – its home position. Many telescopes now contain a Level North Technology (LNT) unit which senses north and the level position automatically. They do this by rotating and tilting the instrument – a procedure which takes a little time and may not be particularly accurate anyway, so many users prefer to bypass this stage and do it manually. The telescope then slews to its first alignment star, which will be one of the brightest in the sky. Your job is now to bring the alignment star to the centre of the field of view, first in the finder and then the main telescope, and once you are happy, press *Enter*. The telescope now finds its second alignment star, you repeat the process, then finally, if everything is OK, the alignment is successful and you can then tell it to seek out any other object in its database.

Celestron's system is SkyAlign, which is incorporated into several telescopes, including the CPC800 shown here. This model includes a GPS unit which avoids the need to set its location and the date and time, but SkyAlign is also available on smaller instruments without GPS, such as the NexStar 114 SLT, costing about £200.

With SkyAlign there is no home position for the telescope. Instead you simply locate any bright star, centre it and press *Enter*, then you drive the instrument to two other bright stars using the handset and repeat the procedure. It doesn't matter that you don't know the names of the stars, or even if they happen to be planets, as long as they are among the 80 brightest objects in the sky. If you have done everything properly, the telescope is now aligned and will find other objects as required.

Yet a third system is adopted by Sky-Watcher in their SynScan controllers. All their mountings are of the type known as German equatorials, about which more later. Unlike the other two systems, you do need a passing acquaintance with the sky in that these mountings must be aligned on the north celestial pole before use. The home position here is with the telescope pointing north and turned so that it is at the top of the mount.

You need to enter the date and time, and also your location. While the other two systems provide lists of locations throughout the world, the SynScan requires you to know your latitude and longitude. Having set it up, the telescope then finds and requires you to centre three bright stars. As with Autostar, if the bright stars it selects are not accessible it will offer alternatives.

▶ *The Sky-Watcher Evostar 80 ED2 PRO is on an EQ5 German mount with the SynScan GO TO system. The telescope is a refractor using special glass that corrects for false colour, and is particularly suited to wide-field astrophotography.*

◀ *The Celestron CPC800 is a 200 mm Schmidt-Cassegrain telescope on fork mounting. It includes GPS and the SkyAlign GO TO system, which involves centring on any three bright stars.*

SUPPLIERS OF THE EQUIPMENT SHOWN HERE

Celestron from David Hinds Ltd, Leighton Buzzard, Beds: www.celestron.uk.com

Meade from Telescope House, Tunbridge Wells, Kent: www.telescopehouse.com

Sky-Watcher from The Widescreen Centre, London W1: www.widescreen-centre.co.uk

All instruments also available from alternative suppliers. Prices quoted here are current as of mid 2008.

▼ *An 80 mm refractor is ideal for wide-field deep-sky photography and also for good close-ups of the Moon, as shown in this photograph of the crater Petavius by Damian Peach, using an inexpensive Philips ToUcam webcam.*

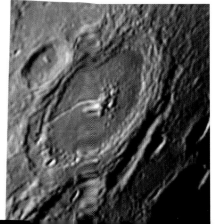

How accurate are GO TO telescopes?

You might hope that a GO TO telescope will find objects for you absolutely precisely, so that they are slap-bang in the middle of the field of view. But this isn't always the case, even when you take great care with the prior alignment of your telescope and centring the alignment stars. There are always slight errors in the manufacture of systems, and a tiny error in positioning will be magnified when you hop from one part of the sky to another and you are viewing a small area of the sky at a magnification of, say, 75 as is typical for even the wide-field eyepiece of a telescope. But you should expect the object to be within the central third of the field of view of the wide-field eyepiece, and experience shows that this is often achieved with each system.

One point to consider is that the telescopes include thousands of objects in their databases, not all of which will be visible with your instrument on the night you are looking. The Meade Autostar controller, for example, contains the same objects whether you are using a 250 mm telescope or an 80 mm. Many of them would be visible with the small telescope from the Mojave Desert, but not from the middle of Middlesbrough, say. Meade also notoriously include some objects that aren't visible at all, such as black holes, in their listing!

Which system is best?

As with most things, it all depends. In terms of accuracy there is not a great deal to choose between them. But individual requirements could play an important part. Both the simpler Meade and the Sky-Watcher systems require you to be able to find north. This might not seem a major problem, but many beginners do find it a challenge, particularly if they don't know the sky at all.

German equatorial mountings, such as those used by Sky-Watcher, are notorious for causing confusion among beginners. In theory, setting one up is simple. However, many beginners really do get tied up in knots by equatorial mounts in general. So, although they have major advantages, as covered later, if you are content with general stargazing it would be better to avoid them. The basic Meade and Celestron mounts are what are called 'altazimuth' mounts, which are simpler to operate.

Meade's automatic system seems very clever. However, the sensors inside the unit are not particularly accurate, and often it will point some way from any bright star. Usually it is obvious which one it wants, but there is often cause for doubt. Sometimes Meade owners find that their instrument just won't align itself after several attempts, while everyone else is already observing. Under these circumstances you just have to resort to choosing the stars for it, which demands some knowledge of the sky.

The Celestron SkyAlign system is particularly suited to beginners since all you need are any three bright stars – or even planets or the Moon – and you don't even need to be able to identify them. However, in tests, SkyAlign would not always work first time and required a repeat alignment.

Taking photos

Many people want to be able to photograph the objects that they view through their telescopes. For the Moon and bright planets, short exposures are all you need, so any mounting that keeps the object steady in the field of view for a few minutes is fine. But if you want to photograph deep-sky objects, such as nebulae and galaxies, you often need exposure times of many minutes. While the basic altazimuth mounts will keep the object centred in the field, the rest of the field of view rotates around them over a period of minutes. So, for long exposures you really do need an equatorially mounted telescope. Fork mounts can often be converted by adding a wedge, which tilts the whole mount at an angle, but many astrophotographers find that the German mounts are more sturdy and less prone to vibration than forks. You can also add a polar alignment telescope to a German mount, which makes aligning the mount on the celestial pole a lot easier. So if you plan to try your hand at deep-sky photography, the Sky-Watcher system may be more convenient for you.

Slight errors in the drive system, known as 'periodic errors', creep in during long-exposure photos, which means using a mount with periodic-error correction (PEC). The system needs to be trained to remember the corrections in advance and, indeed, for accurate GO TO work, most mounts require some user training, which improves their performance. In addition, an autoguiding system is often needed for long-exposure photography.

Are they worth it?

Even many advanced users wouldn't be without their GO TO systems, which take a lot of the guesswork out of finding the right part of the sky. But others point out that relying on a GO TO is a bit like relying on a satnav in the car to get you everywhere – you won't learn your way around for yourself. And the more you rely on power supplies and connections, the more there is to go wrong. Many GO TO instruments are virtually unusable without a power supply, and when that power lead breaks or the batteries run down, it's back to the binoculars!

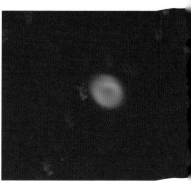

▲ The result of a 7½-minute exposure of the Ring Nebula in Lyra through a 200 mm telescope on an altazimuth mount – the combination of a non-equatorial mount and periodic error in the gears means that stars around the edge of the field of view are trailed into zigzag shapes. Only exposure times of a few seconds are possible without trailing.

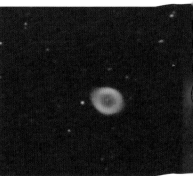

▲ The same object photographed using an equatorial mount corrects for the trailing of the stars. However, very long exposures require additional autoguiding.